How Man
Made Music

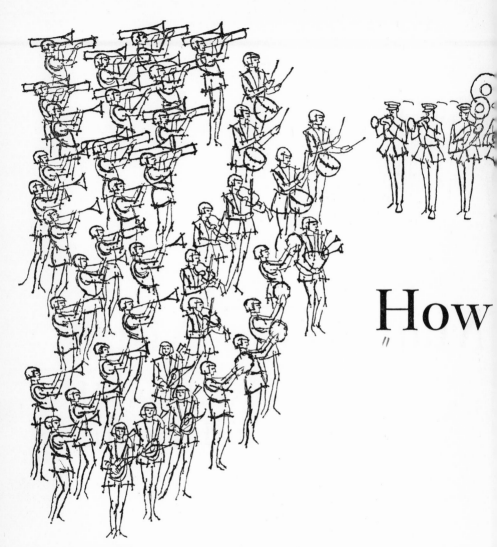

How

Illustrated by Robert William Hinds

Man Made Music

Fannie R. Buchanan
Charles L. Luckenbill

Follett Publishing Company CHICAGO

LIBRARY OF CONGRESS CATALOG CARD NUMBER 59-9448

MANUFACTURED IN THE UNITED STATES OF AMERICA

3456789

Acknowledgements

"How Tribe-Boy Made a Drum" is retold from *Child Life Magazine*. "The Triumph of the Oratorio" quotes newspaper clippings from *The Story of the Oratorio* by Annie Patterson. The late H. W. Matlack of Grinnell College, with Mrs. Matlack, helped to evaluate the book's subject matter. Myrtle E. Parks, Grinnell Cooper School, helped adjust to grade level. Dr. Stanley Korfmacher collaborated in "From Amber to Amplification," Ada Sweezy-Nelson, with Hilda Godfrey Wilson, of Grinnell College Library, Marian Dunham and the staff of Grinnell Steward Library helped with research. Dorothy Robson, Grinnell College Book Store, Elizabeth Mitchell, Business Department of the Grinnell High School, and Barbara Bates Howell helped with book plans and preparation of material.

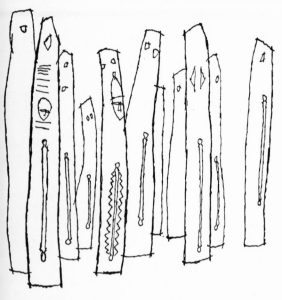

Prelude

IN LEARNING to make music, man had to achieve two things: he had to think up the music and to sound it out. *How Man Made Music* tells the exciting story of how man perfected his ability to "dream" music into being and his art of "sounding it out."

The story begins with earliest man, who somehow and somewhere began to sing and to make songs. How he made this music was a mystery to him. Surely, like the sunlight and the moonlight, music must be a gift from the gods!

In striking wood against stone, in beating a hollow log with a club, in blowing into a hollow horn, man found that he could make instruments that would help him sound out his music.

But how man "thought up" music is the difficult and marvelous achievement. To get an insight into this phase of the story, we walk in the rain with Dan Emmett and feel the rhythm of "Dixie" begin to stir in his mind. We stand in a little attic with Joseph Haydn

while he puzzles over the first designs of the modern sonata form. And we are on a ship at sea when Richard Wagner gets his inspiration for *The Flying Dutchman*.

As we read, there steals upon us a feeling of the oneness of the great human family. Music patterns change, but the fullest moments of man's life have always been lived to music. Whenever he has delighted greatly, grieved sorely, loved deeply, laughed freely, or prayed sincerely, he has called upon music to lend wings to his voice. And as long as he is capable of reaching these spiritual heights and depths, man will always make music.

Max V. Exner

Extension Music Specialist
Iowa State College
Ames, Iowa

Contents

ONE

From Shouting to Song

Man Begins to Make Music

MUSIC BELONGS equally to everybody. The paper boy, biking along his dawn beat, whistles a tune; and the President of the United States whistles the same melody on the White House lawn. A baritone sings a thrilling aria before a Metropolitan Opera audience; and a policeman, on his night patrol, hums the same music. Classical or popular, many are the songs that man whistles, hums, or sings in his work and play.

Music expresses man's inmost feelings; it is the "language which speaks without words." What are some of the many ways in which it "speaks"? The background music in movies helps to tell the story, to express emotion. In radio and television, it marks a change of scene and prepares the listener for what is coming next.

WHAT POWER HAS MUSIC?

History is marked with incidents that tell of the mysterious power of music. Time and again a drum, a bugle, or a song has rallied retreating troops to victory.

During World War II General Jonathan Wainwright and his men were moved from one Japanese prison camp to another in the Philippines. In their long months of captivity they had no word as to how the war was going. For all they knew, the United States might have fared as badly as the Philippines. One morning, weary, weak, and discouraged, they trudged along a road — going they knew not where, facing they knew not what. Then, clear, crisp as a fife, a tune rang out. Heads lifted, eyes brightened. Without words, a tattered little Filipino lad, standing on the roadside, whistled a message to the soldiers. Wobbly legs straightened, sagging shoulders squared. The flag — their flag — still waved "O'er the land of the free and the home of the brave."

In the Bible or in the records of modern medicine, one can read of the strange healing power of music. King Saul was terrified by a mysterious illness. His servants sent for a young musician, David, who "took an harp and played — and Saul was well." Today, in our mental hospitals, music plays an important role in the treatment of patients.

12

Where does the story of music, which has such powers of uplifting man's spirit, of healing his body, begin? How did man begin to make music? The story begins with the earliest man, who somehow and somewhere began to sing and to make songs. How he made this music was a mystery to him. It was mysterious, like the sunlight and the moonlight, which he believed were gifts from his gods to make him happy. Yet music was even nearer than sunshine; it came from within man himself. Surely, it, too, must be a gift from the gods!

Primitive man learned and copied from Nature. The first home builder got ideas from arching caves and tree boughs. The first printer, writing in sign language, copied a tree, a bird, the sun, and other things he wished to represent. The first artist drew pictures of the plants and animals he saw about him.

However, the first maker of tunes had nothing visible to copy. True, he could hear the sounds of wind and water, the songs of birds and insects. But these musical sounds were constantly moving. And so the first music of primitive man had to have motion also. For a tune is made up of sounds that move with rhythm and melody. It cannot be stopped or held for examination. When a tune stops moving, or flowing, it ceases to be a tune. It becomes a noise — a sound without rhythm and melody.

HOW DOES MUSIC DIFFER FROM NOISE?

When the early tribesman beat a signal on a hollow stump-drum, he began to change noise into music, for there had to be rhythm to his signaling. He must have worked out a code using strong and weak beats. Perhaps STRONG-weak, STRONG-weak, STRONG-weak signaled BIG-beast, BIG-beast, BIG-beast. This is the same rhythm used when cheerleaders shout RAH-rah, RAH-rah, RAH-rah, JOHN-son!

When the tribesman struck his hollow drum like this: STRONG-weak-weak, STRONG-weak-weak, STRONG-weak-weak, perhaps he meant EL-e-phant, EL-e-phant, EL-e-phant. The cheerleader also uses this rhythm: RAH-rah-rah, RAH-rah-rah, RAH-rah-rah, DICK-in-son!

WHAT MAKES RHYTHM?

Such regular repetitions of strong beats contrasted with weak beats make the difference between cheering and mob-yelling. This repetition of accents gives rhythm to any sound. And rhythm is a necessary part of music. It is the heartbeat of music!

But a tune has melody as well as rhythm. The RAH-rah-rah of the cheerleader moves from accent to accent and is all on the same tone. A melody moves from accent to accent, but it also moves from tone to tone: MY-*country,* TIS-*of thee,* SWEET-*land-of,* LIB-er-ty moves from tone to tone and makes the melody for one of the world's best-known songs.

Of course, primitive men thought nothing about rhythm or melody. Their war songs roared as defiantly as the jungle lion. Their death chants wailed as moanfully as the autumn winds. Their love songs trilled as wistfully as the mating call of a bird.

Perhaps the first songs began when men "shouted for joy" over the capture of some fierce beast of prey or some tribal enemy. When the story of the capture was told around a campfire, perhaps the shouts were repeated and finally grew into a chanted refrain. The first war songs may have started with defiant shouts to encourage the warriors. Later, when the warriors shouted their war cries in their stories of a battle, the listeners may have echoed the cries to make the story more interesting.

The early people, as people do today, enjoyed such story hours around their campfires. Legends of long ago describe men who made a business of storytelling. Before man learned to write, these storytellers were historians. Their tales, handed down through the generations, became mixed with myths and legends. Some stories have survived even to this day.

WHO WERE THE BARDS?

As men banded together and formed clans and kingdoms, the storytellers, or bards, made a living by spinning their tales. Food, lodging, and gifts came from their listeners, so the bards tried to make their stories as interesting as possible. In time they made their stories into poems, or "lays," which they sang to the accompaniment of a small hand-harp.

A singing storyteller, or minstrel, was the most welcome guest at a castle gate. Everyone from the prince to the goatherd came to greet him. All assembled in the great hall to listen to his tales.

15

Even during warfare a minstrel was freely admitted to any camp. His songs and his harp were his "passport." An interesting spy story of long ago tells how King Alfred the Great, disguised as a musician, went to the camp of the enemy Danes. He wandered as he liked among the warriors. When he had the information he wanted, he wandered out of camp, still singing his "lay." He left with his harp but returned with his sword and army to drive the Danes out of England.

Bards in their travels brought more than tales. They gathered news and opinions of other people and spread them from one isolated community to another. An old story of the British Isles shows how highly bards were regarded. It tells that a king might wear seven colors in his dress, a bard six, lords and ladies five, a governor of a fortress four, gentlemen three, soldiers two, and the common folk only one.

While bards were making story-songs, people outside camp and castle were singing, too. They made songs for their dances, their feasts, and even for everyday incidents.

HOW DID SOME EARLY SONGS BEGIN?

A mother crooned a little tune to her baby. Perhaps another mother added words as she sang her sleepy little tune. Thus she crooned the first lullaby. It has been said that a mother was the first singer and the first song was a lullaby.

Indian lore helps to show how early songs began. In some Indian tribes today the Indian mother sings an age-old lullaby. She croons the word *wi-um* (we̅-um) over and over

16

as she gently rocks the cradleboard to which her papoose is bound.

The Indian sings to the dawn, to the stars, to the rain. He has made a song for hunting, for planting, for harvesting. He has one about his pipe, his friend, his enemy, and even his burial. These are old, old tribal songs that have been passed down from father to son for many generations. They are sung in a manner that makes the repeated tones more like noise than music. They are almost the only examples in existence of the songs of primitive man. They show how music changes as man changes.

HOW DO OUR MUSICIANS USE INDIAN TUNES?

American musicians have sometimes used Indian tunes in their compositions. To these they have added music of their own. A song of an old Indian mother mourning her lost son is one of the themes, or little tunes, that MacDowell used in his funeral march, "From an Indian Lodge." To the Indian tune MacDowell added chords of sad, heavy music that throb like the slow beat of tom-toms. Undoubtedly, the Indian mother would like her own song better. But many listeners feel that MacDowell's music expresses more than the lament of one mother; it pictures the tragedy of the vanishing Indian race.

Two popular songs made from Indian flute calls are "The Land of the Sky-blue Water," by Cadman, and "By the Waters of Minnetonka," by Lieurance. The words of these songs are old tribal legends retold in poetry to be sung to primitive Indian tunes. Both composers made the original flute calls longer and more interesting by adding tones that could not be played on a crude Indian flute. To this melody the composers fitted the harmony of an accompaniment which helps the tune, and the words retell the old story.

In eight short lines the Cadman song beautifully tells the story of an Indian maiden who had been carried away as a captive from the "land of the sky-blue waters." Her beauty and her bravery win the admiration of one of her captors. In early dawning he goes to her lodge to serenade her in the tribal manner with his home-made flute and love call. But the beautiful captive, homesick for her sky-blue lakes, does not answer to his wooing.

The Indian of today does not approve of his calls being "made over." A young Dakota brave heard a flutist play the melody of "By the Waters of Minnetonka." In the Indian manner, he turned away with one word, "Ruined!" He wanted his music left just as the tribesman had made it to express his inmost feelings.

WHY IS OUR MUSIC MORE COMPLICATED?

But the modern music maker and the modern listener, long since passed from the tribal stage, want more and different tones in the melodies they sing, the music they listen to. Man's songs today, like his life, have greater variety than those of primitive man. He associates with many people and learns to think and act agreeably with them. He wants his tones blending with other tones in what is called harmony. He makes songs with soprano, alto, tenor, and bass parts for large groups to sing together. Besides variety, he wants "bigness" in his choruses, orchestras, and bands.

His speech and his music express finer feelings than

those of primitive man. He has passed the shouting stage. Now he sings — now he makes music to express the beautiful, the good, the noble sentiments within his soul. Truly such music may be called Divine!

TWO

From Hollow Stump to Drum

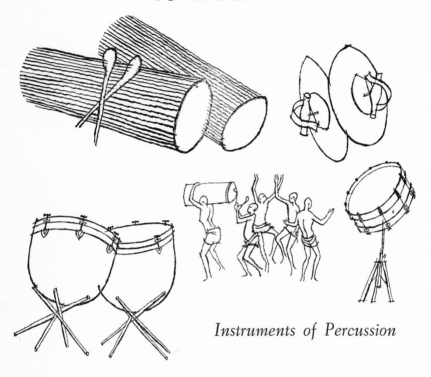

Instruments of Percussion

EVERY standard musical instrument has a nickname to tell how it is played. It is either a Banger, a Blower, a Picker, or a Scraper. In a large orchestra, different kinds play together. There it is fairly easy to discover in which class each instrument belongs. The drums are not the only Bangers nor the horns the only Blowers. The golden harp looks too splendid to be called a Picker; but even so, the harpist sets the strings to singing by plucking them with the fingers. Because violin strings are rubbed by the bow, even this king of instruments must answer to the nickname of Scraper.

WHAT KIND OF INSTRUMENT IS THE OLDEST?

Bangers, which properly are called percussion instruments, are probably the oldest of all because they were easily made. They had their beginning back in the times when man was making his first crude tools. All primitive people had Bangers. They clapped pieces of wood together. They struck wood against stone. They beat hollow logs with clubs. They made rattles of dried gourds and pebbles. These different kinds of sounds were the beginning of music. They pleased the tribesman and helped him to express feelings he could express in no other way.

One day man discovered that striking a tightly stretched dried skin gave him another kind of sound. He began to invent drums. When he learned to work with metal, he found that by striking it he could make still another new sound. He began to make Bangers of metal.

But the drum was his great invention. He probably began by covering a hollow stump with a stretched skin. Some accident must have given him this idea. How it really happened may only be guessed. Drums as large as hollow stumps or as small as toys are older than man's oldest records.

FOR WHAT PURPOSES WERE DRUMS USED?

Early drums were used for giving signals or alarms. In the wild life of the jungle such a loud-voiced messenger was

21

sure to be important. Of course, the tribesman kept on trying to improve it.

The chief would want to carry the drum with him on the warpath. It would frighten the enemy. It would signal his own men. A portable drum must be made. To do this perhaps he burned a hollow in a piece of log and covered it with a stretched skin. Perhaps he fastened a skin over half a dried gourd. Perhaps he made some sort of hoop or ring to hold a stretched skin as it is held in a tambourine. It is certain that such hand drums were used in very early times.

Drums were also used in the tribal dances, important events among primitive people even today. Instead of offering prayers, many tribes performed sacred dances to their gods: sun dances when they needed sunshine; rain dances when they needed rain; hunting dances when they needed meat; feast dances when they were thankful; war dances when they were going to battle. These ceremonial dances were performed to the rhythmic sound of the drum. Primitive man tried to please his gods by making the best dance he could. To make a better dance, he had to make a better drum.

HOW MANY KINDS OF DRUMS DO WE HAVE?

Thousands and thousands of years have passed since the time of the booming hollow stump. Men have made drums of many shapes and sizes. Yet, after all, among the old ones and the new ones there are only three different kinds. These three kinds were invented long, long ago by men whose tribes have been forgotten and whose race cannot now be traced. They may have a stretched skin over a hollow shell, as the kettle drum has; they may have two skins, one stretched over each end of a hollow cylinder, as the bass and the snare drums have; or they may have one skin stretched over an open frame, as the tambourine has.

WHY ARE THE KETTLEDRUMS IMPORTANT?

These three old kinds of drum are now made in several new ways. The kettledrum, which began with the hollow stump, is the most important. Today its body is a big kettle of shiny copper. The calfskin parchment that covers it is almost transparent. Instead of being held in place by weights or stones, as the skin of the stump drum was, it is held by a metal ring. This will tighten or loosen the parchment, and in this way the drum can be tuned to the pitch of other instruments. This is why the kettledrums are so important. They are played in pairs, or in groups of three or more, because with two drums a skillful player can sound any tone in the scale. The kettledrums are called the *timpani*.

The tribesman beat his hollow stump with a club. The timpani man has several kinds of drumsticks. He has flat-headed ones of felt with a whalebone button at the tip. He has wooden ones padded with sponge and with rubber. He knows the sound each kind will make. Not only can he beat out the BOOM-boom-boom of the stump drum, but he also can make his drum roar like lions or tremble like the bleating of a timid fawn. He can express a feeling of shuddering horror or of mystery that cannot be explained by words. Through all the past centuries how man must have worked to perfect a drum that can express such different feelings!

23

The bass drum, like those early tribal Bangers, does not really make music, but it helps man to express his feelings by adding rhythm to tones of other instruments. Just hearing its BOOM-boom-boom makes a person feel brave. The bass drum of olden days was very heavy. Today its large hooplike body is made of aluminum, with a skin over each end. Its weight is so slight that even a schoolboy can carry it to beat the steady rhythm of a marching band. Sometimes the bass drum in an orchestra helps to tell a music story by imitating thunder or a roaring cannon, although it is usually just a timekeeper.

HOW IS THE SNARE DRUM DIFFERENT?

The snare drum looks like a baby bass drum, but it has an entirely different sound. Of course, being much smaller, it would not have such a booming voice. But size is not the secret of the snare drum's crisp rattling tones. It always seems to say, "I'm excited! I'm excited! Step lively! Step lively!" The snare drummer uses two round-tipped sticks of hard wood. He plays on one end of the drum only. The other end explains the secret of its exciting voice. Some inventor once stretched two strings made of dried membrane across the lower end. When the upper end is struck, these strings (snares) vibrate against the skin of the lower end. This gives the snare drum its name and its exciting sound.

The famous talking drums of Africa are used by expert native drummers to beat out code messages. These messages are relayed from village to village through miles of jungle and forest. Students of primitive music have found it impossible to put into notation the rapidly changing rhythms used, nor can modern symbols as yet indicate the changes of tempo and the expressive control of volume, all of which enter into the code transmission.

The little tambourine is the gypsy drum. It is a small, wooden hoop with a membrane stretched over one end. It has little metal jangles wired to the sides. In the Bible story about the children of Israel, this kind of instrument is called a *timbrel*. Miriam, the sister of Moses, used to sing and dance to its gay, jangling sound.

WHAT OTHER BANGERS DO WE HAVE?

Besides drums, man has made many other musical Bangers that do not play tunes. There are the little castanets, which are only timekeepers. But they have such a quick, rhythmic clack that they can make a tune more interesting. Long ago they were tribal rattlebones. The name castanet is Spanish and means chestnut wood. In Spain the first castanets were made from the chestnut tree. The Spanish gypsies made them after hearing the wooden clackers that were brought into Spain by the conquering Moors from Africa. Castanets are a pair of little wooden, spoon-shaped shells, tied loosely on a cord.

Negroes from Africa brought rattlebones to America. The end man in a minstrel show is still called "the bones." His funny songs are sung to the rhythmic taps of two pieces of rib-bone-shaped wood.

The nickname Bangers surely belongs to the cymbals. For thousands of years they have helped the drums beat out rhythm. They look very simple, just brass hammered into two big, slightly hollowed disks. A strap by which to grasp them is fastened to the center of each. But they are not so easily made. Man had to experiment with metal for many years before his cymbals had a bright, clear tone. The Turks are said to have made the best cymbals. It is not known how they combined the metals used in making them. Although cymbals have a banging sound, men long ago discovered they should not be clashed together. Instead, the player should bring the edges together with a sliding motion. Cymbals help to make exciting music. They are heard in the music of "In the Hall of the Mountain King" when the home of the Trolls is destroyed.

The gong is another instrument that does not play tunes but helps make special kinds of music. It comes from China, where it is used in temple service. It is a large, thin plate made from an alloy of different metals skillfully melted together. When it is brushed or rubbed by a soft drumstick, it makes a weird, mysterious sound, which can be increased to a really terrifying roar.

ON WHAT BANGERS CAN TUNES BE PLAYED?

The people of China have many Bangers. They use stones, metal, skin, wood, and baked earth to make the most surprising musical sounds. An old legend tells that long ago a myth boy showed the Chinese Emperor how to make music

26

from stones. He selected 16 of a certain kind, and cut and shaped them until each one sounded a different tone. He then made wonderful music by tapping the stones with a little mallet. The Emperor named this instrument the *king*. Regardless of how the singing stones were discovered, it is true that for more than 4,000 years the king has been the favorite instrument among the Chinese.

The marimba of Mexico and the xylophone of Russia may be second cousins of the king, for they are also Bangers that play melodies. These are made of carefully tuned bars of very hard wood and, like the king, are played with a little mallet. There is a sound box or set of tubes under the bars to make the tone stronger.

Instead of being made by emperors and fairy folk, perhaps these tone-making Bangers are only the descendants of the wooden and the stone clappers used by ancient tribesmen. What would one of those boys of long ago think if he heard a modern xylophone?

WHAT IS A CARILLON?

The most loved of all Bangers are the bells of many kinds, sizes, and descriptions. They are found in every country of the world. Big bells to call people to church and to school; little bells to jingle on the circus clowns' caps; middle-sized bells to hang around the neck of the bell-cow so the owner may know where to find his herd; clock bells to strike hours; buoy bells to warn sailors at sea; telephone bells, train bells, sleigh bells, doorbells, and, best of all, tower bells hung in sets which not only chime musically but upon which tunes can be played.

Such a set of bells is called a *carillon*. The famous carillon of the Bok Tower at Lake Wales, Florida, has 61 tuned bells. The largest one weighs 22,000 pounds, and the smallest weighs 16 pounds. The bells hang in rows, the smaller ones at the top. They are sounded by levers moved by the bell ringer. No wonder this is called the Singing Tower and people go there from far and near to hear the bell concerts. There are many such sets of bells in the Old World. The saying, "the towers of Holland sing," has become a proverb among travelers, because almost every city of this little country has its own wonderful carillon.

HOW CAN ORCHESTRAS USE BELLS?

In an orchestra the sound of these great sets of tuned bells is imitated by a set of tuned metal tubes called orchestra chimes. There is also a German instrument called the *glockenspiel,* which sounds like a tuned set of little bells.

In the music of *The Nutcracker Suite* the French *celesta* plays for "The Dance of the Sugar Plum Fairy." This instrument sounds like a fairy carillon and looks like a baby piano. It is really a set of steel plates arranged in a tiny piano-like case. When the keys are pressed, small hammers sound tuned plates of steel. One famous musician described the music as "divinely beautiful!"

WHEN MAY STRINGED INSTRUMENTS BE CALLED BANGERS?

Who would ever call a stringed instrument a Banger? But strings may be struck, as well as picked and scraped. The oldest string Banger on record is the *dulcimer* of the Old Testament stories. In a picture of an Assyrian king who lived hundreds of years before the birth of Jesus, the dulcimer is shown hanging about his neck. One hand strikes the strings with a hammer, while the other hand is pressed against the strings to muffle or to stop the sound.

The *cembalo*, which is heard in Hungarian orchestras and in gypsy camps, is one descendant of the dulcimer. But the *piano* is the most famous relative of this ancient instrument. Open the wooden case, and there are the strings. Press the keys, and felt hammers fly up and strike them. Look carefully and see that a felt "muffler" is there with a lever to press it against the string when the tone is to be stopped.

WHAT OTHER INSTRUMENT WAS THE ANCESTOR OF THE PIANO?

It took hundreds of years for the piano to develop from the old-time dulcimer. The piano's story involves minstrels and monks, musicians and mechanics, kings and queens, inventors, metalworkers, and many a man with an imagination. The minstrels who wandered about from country to country carried the dulcimer and its relatives of the East to the singers of the West. The monks in the monasteries invented keyboards for their *organs*. Inventors and mechanics borrowed this new idea and made a *clavichord* (*clavis* — a key; *chord* — a string). This might be called the great-great-grandmother of the piano. Musicians complained that its tones were too soft. Inventors tried to find ways to improve the instrument.

Kings and noblemen gladly gave their help. In those times each court had its own orchestra, and its concerts were as popular as today's television shows. And a new kind of instrument caused as much interest as a new television or movie actor does today. Everyone talked about the clavichord!

At last, after many experiments and many failures, an Italian invented a clavichord that could play either loud or very soft music. In Italian the word for soft is *piano,* and the word for loud is *forte.* So he called his instrument the *piano-forte.*

WHAT WAS DONE TO IMPROVE THE PIANO?

But still men worked for more than a hundred years before the piano was perfected. They made strings of wire that could be stretched tightly. They made a frame of steel that could stand the tension of the strings. They improved the hammers, the mufflers, and the keys. They invented pedals. They made square pianos, upright pianos, grand pianos. The piano of today sounds 88 different tones. It has 243 strings. The steel frame that holds these tightly stretched strings must withstand a pull or strain of 30 tons.

The piano and other Bangers have been vastly improved since their early beginnings. Today they can still be jolly and noisy, but they are also makers of music. They have grown up to deserve their proper musical name — "Instruments of Percussion."

How Tribe-Boy
Made a Drum

A Mysterious Voice

Tribe-Boy did not look like the boys of today. He had long, shaggy hair; his fingernails were heavy and sharp, like claws; his skin was tanned and coarse.

Instead of a suit such as boys today wear, Tribe-Boy wore the striped skin of a great snake hanging from one of his shoulders. The other tribeschildren wore skins of animals. On one was the spotted skin of a hyena; another wore the grayish-yellow skin of a jackal. Some wore short skirts of woven rushes. All were barelegged, with sandals of hide in place of shoes.

At night, the tribeschildren slept in caves. For food they ate berries and nuts and flesh of wild beasts that the men of the tribe killed. They tore the flesh into bits with their strong fingers. They gnawed the bones with their sharp teeth.

Sometimes the tribespeople would have a feast. While the meat cooked in an open fire, the young men of the tribe would dance in a circle around it. The women of the tribe kept time for the dancers. They clapped their hands and beat sticks together. This was their only music.

Then, quite by chance, the first great drum was made, and Tribe-Boy found out that it could furnish music for the dancers. This is how it came about:

The tribesmen had speared a large antelope. The tribeswomen wanted the strong skin to make sandals for the tribeschildren. With sharp stone tools they scraped off the hair. Then the skin had to be dried out. Where should they stretch it?

31

Nearby was a big hollow stump that the tribeswomen used for a barrel. Into it they put food they wished to keep. They covered the food with small stones to keep it safe from squirrels and other animals. That day the hollow stump was empty. Its edges had become worn and smooth. It would make a good drying frame. The tribeswomen spread the skin over it, and with strong sinews they tied stone weights to the corners to hold it in place.

Day after day the sun took up the moisture from the skin. As it became dry, it grew smaller, but the weights still held it. Soon it was very tight across the top of the stump.

One afternoon the women were roasting a wild boar. Back from the fire, the men sat around the tribal chief. The chief was very old, but he was still tall and straight. His eyes were keen and bright. The tribesmen knew that he was wise and clever. It was he alone who should wear the splendid striped skin of the jungle tiger; it was he alone, of all the tribe, who should have the bright feather of the flamingo for his headdress.

The tribeschildren were playing about the hollow stump. Tribe-Boy was with them. The tribeschildren liked his games. He was much more clever than they. He was tall and straight like the chief. Tribe-Boy was proud of his strong arm. "See," he said, "it is so that I killed the big snake!" He raised his stick for a great stroke. As it came down, it struck the tight skin across the hollow stump.

Boom! The sound echoed through the jungle!

Tribe-Boy sprang back from the stump. The tribeschildren cried out in terror. The tribesmen and women came running to find out what the great sound might be. The children could not tell them. They pointed to the stump. They pointed to Tribe-Boy.

The old chief asked him questions. "What made the loud cry?" But Tribe-Boy could only tell that the great voice had come from the hollow stump. Some strange wild creature must be hiding there. At last, to show the old chief, Tribe-Boy again brought the stick down on the stretched skin.

Boom!

The children shrieked and ran to their mothers. The men grasped their spears and clubs and formed in a line between the women and the crying stump. They were sure that some fierce beast was crouching there under the skin. They stood waiting for it to spring out upon them. But the skin did not move. There was no sound from the hollow stump.

After a while the men came closer. They saw the stone weights that held the skin in place. The strange beast was trapped! Then there was great rejoicing. The young men danced to celebrate the capture of the loud-voiced animal. As they passed the stump some of the most daring struck the skin to make the creature cry out. At this the children covered their ears; the old men shook their heads; the women were too frightened to clap for the dancers.

Back from the others, beside the old chief, Tribe-Boy stood watching. Suddenly he had an idea. Grasping his stick, he sprang through the circle. He bounded close to the stump. He struck the skin, and the voice boomed in answer. Tribe-Boy stood his ground. He struck the skin time after time, and time after time, to each stroke, the voice answered.

The men stopped their dance to watch. The children stopped their crying to listen. The eyes of the old chief followed every motion of Tribe-Boy's stick.

Then Tribe-Boy began to beat in rhythm as he had heard the tribeswomen clap for the dancers. And the voice answered in rhythm, time and again, "boom, Boom-boom-boom! boom, Boom-boom-boom!"

33

The young men liked this. They shouted aloud and sprang into a circle-dance about the stump. The women liked it, too. They laughed and chattered and began to clap, keeping time to the booming. The children and the old men gathered about.

Suddenly the old chief sprang into the circle, leaping and bounding in time to the booming. The long tail of his tiger skin lashed his ankles, and the bright feathers of his headdress waved wildly. How the men shouted! It was long since the old chief had danced in the circle! But now he was young again. He sprang into the air like the cliff kids; he turned and whirled like the tree squirrel! The tribeschildren had never seen such dancing. They clapped and stamped with their mothers. Tribe-Boy beat faster and faster.

At last the wild dance ended. The tired dancers dropped to the ground. But the old chief came to where Tribe-Boy stood beside the speaking stump. "You are very brave," he said. "You shall be the keeper of this great voice. For you it shall speak to make old hearts young, dull eyes sparkle, and heavy feet light." From his own hair he took the flamingo feather, and placed it in the matted hair of Tribe-Boy. "You are very brave," he said. "For you the voice shall speak, and the people will love it."

That night, while the tribespeople slept, Tribe-Boy sat alone beside the hollow stump. If only he might see this hidden creature! "It has not moved," he said to himself. "It has not moved. It is sleeping. I must see it."

He caught up a torch from the fire and fastened it into the crotch of a tree above him. With his strong fingers he loosened the heavy weights. "I must, I must see this strange creature that speaks for the dancing—"

But when he lifted the skin, holding the torch for light, there was only the empty hollow of the stump! Then Tribe-Boy's hands trembled as the tiny fronds of the tree fern do when the little rains touch them. His sturdy limbs shook as the tall palm does when the roaring wind sweeps the jungle. He crouched beside the empty stump.

Far off in the sky there came a flash of lightning. Tribe-Boy caught the roll of distant thunder. He lifted his head. Here, too, was a great voice. Many times he had heard it speak, yet always from the air above, where his eyes could find no creature. Was the voice of the hollow stump a child of this greater hidden voice that only spoke from behind the clouds? If he covered the stump would the booming voice speak for him again?

Tribe-Boy sprang to his feet. He replaced the skin. He fastened the stone weights. At last, when the stretched skin again covered the hollow stump, Tribe-Boy seized his stick, and, half afraid, he tapped the skin gently. The voice answered softly.

Tribe-Boy dropped to his knees beside the hollow stump. Throwing his arms across the stretched skin, he pressed his cheek close against it. "You are there," he cried softly, "you are there. I may not see you, but I shall keep you, and you shall speak for me, and my people shall love you!"

How the tribes found that any hollow stump or hollow bowl, if it be covered by a tightly stretched skin, will hold the voice of the drum, we may never know. There are no books old enough to tell us. But this we do know, that as the stump-drum spoke for Tribe-Boy long ago, the drums still speak for us today. Their voices still make old hearts young, dull eyes sparkle, and heavy feet grow light; and the people still love them.

THREE

From Ram's Horn
to Trumpet

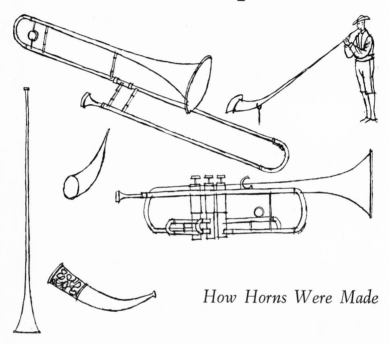

How Horns Were Made

THE school band is marching up the street. Its horns of brass
and of silver flash brightly in the sunlight. Its music sets the
air ringing. With heads high the players step proudly.
Passers-by stand to watch them. All along the street, spines
straighten and chins go up. The horns are calling out their
age-old challenge, "Attention!" All who hear become alert.
The sound of a horn has always made people stop and listen.

In the days before man learned to make bowls of clay, he used an animal horn from which to drink. No story is old enough to tell when or how man first discovered that the hollow horn or tusk of a wild animal could make a startling sound. But there are very ancient stories that show how these have long been used to give commanding signals. In drinking, the large end was raised to the lips. How did primitive man get the idea of turning the horn about and blowing into the small end? Perhaps the story might have been like this:

HOW MIGHT MAN HAVE LEARNED TO BLOW A HORN?

Some tribesman had an especially fine drinking horn. It was long and slender. He had polished it inside and outside by rubbing it with sand and pebbles. He prized it greatly. In some way the tip became broken. He was looking it over as a boy would examine a broken knife. By chance he put the tip to his lips and blew into it. Then came a most surprising blast of sound. From near and far the tribespeople came running. What a wonderful signal! A great discovery had been made!

But blowing a horn is not always as easy as that. To produce horn tones the lips and the breath must be used in very special ways. The tribesman had a horn that was well shaped. He happened to press his lips into the opening in just the right way. When he blew it again, perhaps the sound did not come at all. Perhaps many days and even seasons passed before those primitive men learned which horns were best. They had to learn, too, how the lips help to make the horn signal. Yet in some way man did learn how to produce certain tones from these animal horns.

The natural tones of a well-shaped horn are *do, do above, sol above*. Horns that sounded these three tones were the easiest to blow. These tones became so familiar that a horn that did not produce them was considered coarse and unpleasant. Sometimes a skillful blower with an unusually long horn could sound even a fourth tone, the second *do above*. Such horns were highly prized and were passed on from generation to generation. Through hundreds of years, they became the foundation of the *do-re-mi* scale that every schoolboy knows.

As primitive man learned to use tools and to work with wood and metal, he found ways to improve his signal horn. He found that the largest and longest horn would sound the best signal because a long, hollow tube sounds a better, clearer tone than a short one. He invented mouthpieces of different shapes to fit into the tip of his horn. These helped his lips to make the tones stronger. He lengthened the tube by adding other pieces of horn. This helped him to make the tones more certain. Using wood and metal, he made horns with very long tubes. These would sound the tone *mi* above the highest *do* of the old tubes. Some of the ancient horns were so long that when they were used, the flaring end, or bell as it is called, had to be supported on a rack or a stand.

WHAT HORNS DID THE ISRAELITES HAVE?

An old, old Bible story of the Jewish people tells of two such horns. (Numbers, 10th chapter.) In the story they are spoken of as trumpets. Moses used them for signals while he was guiding the children of Israel through the wilderness into the promised land. These signal horns were made of solid silver, and must have been very long, and have had very powerful voices. The signals were heard by the thousands of Israelites in their camps. When one trumpet sounded, all the princes came together in a central meeting place. When both trumpets sounded, all the people gathered in one assembly. The old story also explains that when the trumpets sounded an "alarm," all the people knew that they were to break camp and move forward.

This story helps to prove that thousands of years ago man had already learned to make metal horns with which different signals could successfully be given, although only a few tones could be sounded.

Shepherds in mountain countries of the Old World still use wooden horns 15 or 16 feet long. The flaring end, or bell, rests upon the ground as the shepherd plays his herd call. The tones echo down the valleys and up among the peaks. Other shepherds hear and answer. Each shepherd has his own call made up from the few tones his horn can sound.

Even in very ancient times there were many shapes and sizes of horns. The Knights of King Arthur's Court carried ivory ones made from elephant tusks. These were called *oliphants.* They were beautifully carved and decorated. In those days of knighthood, when there were many nobles, each with his own great estate, every landowner had his own horn call. When lands changed owners, this call was part of the formal ceremony. Villages then had a town horn in place of the sirens used today. When stagecoaches came into use, the post horn was always sounded with a flourish as the coach drew up to the tavern door. These coach or post horns were much like the bugles now used in Drum and Bugle Corps of grade schools. The best of them could sound *do, mi,* and *sol.*

Long ago, fox hunting was a most popular sport among the aristocracy. Then every countryside had its famous hunter. Over his scarlet coat he wore his fox horn hanging by a cord about his shoulder. Hunting horns were longer and more slender than the post horns. They could sound five tones, *do, do above, sol above, do above, mi above.* Some extra-long ones would even sound a higher *do.*

WHAT DID MEN DO WITH EXTRA LONG HORNS?

How could a hunter ride through the forest with such a horn swinging at his side? He managed it in this way: by experimenting he found that a tube may be curved without changing its tone. He coiled the long slender horn into a big circle through which he slipped his head and his right arm. The circle rested on his left shoulder. The flare was behind and the mouthpiece in front, where it could be lifted easily to the lips.

Now that several tones of different pitch could be sounded from his horn, the hunter began to make different calls. Each master of the chase had his own signal by which he could tell his mates how the hunt was going. First, there was the "Call to the Chase"; then, the call to tell that a fresh track had been found; the "View Halloo" was sounded when the fox was sighted; the "Mort" told that the fox had been taken. There were also different calls for different animals.

All this meant that the horns were being made better. The tube had now become so long that it was worn in a double coil about the shoulders of the hunter. Because more tones could be sounded, the hunters began to make up fancy calls and longer tunes to express their joy after a successful chase. In this way the horn began to make music as well as signals. It was learning to sing as well as to shout.

HOW DID MEN GET MORE NOTES FROM A HORN?

In the early days when two horns were used together to give one signal, they were of different lengths. A shorter tube always sounds a higher tone than a long one. This is why a signal using two horns would easily be distinguished from a signal sounded on one horn. Then some clever tribes-man invented a way to make his one horn sound the tones of both a long and a short tube. This is the way he did it. He cut a small hole in the side of his long horn. This had the effect of shortening the tube and made his long horn sound the tones of a short horn. When he pressed his finger tightly over the hole and closed it, his horn gave its original tones. This was a great invention.

WHY ARE HORNS CURVED AND COILED?

Through hundreds of years man worked at this idea and improved upon it. Horns were made with as many holes as a player had fingers with which to cover them. What a lot of experimenting was required to find just where to place these useful finger holes! When at last they were located in just the right positions to produce the tones wanted, the tube of the horn had to be curved and coiled to bring the holes within reach of the player's fingers. One of the old-time horns of this kind, which had six finger holes, was called the *serpent*. In order to bring the holes within reach of the player, the tube had to be curved in and out in much the shape of a wriggling snake.

All this time, and for hundreds of years after, horns were being made in many different ways. At last they were really singing instruments. Some kinds were not so good as others. The poor ones would be used for a time and then would be laid aside and forgotten as the old serpent-horn had been. But the best kinds were gradually made better in every way.

OF WHAT USE ARE VALVES?

The greatest improvement came through the invention of valves, which can make the tube shorter or longer at the touch of a finger on a key or lever. By the use of such valves the best of the old signal horns became singing horns and are found in the bands and orchestras of today. These do not look at all like the first signal horns, but if the brass tubes are uncoiled and straightened out they are found to have the tapering shape of the old-time animal horn. But of course they are many times longer and the flare is much wider than ever grew upon the head of any animal.

The trumpet and the trombone do not have this tapering shape. They have slender tubes that do not flare until the abrupt spread of the bell. For this reason they are called trumpets instead of horns.

The trumpet is the "Old Warrior" of the music world. All the great battles of history are in its story; all the pride of victory is in its strong, confident voice. If its slender tube were uncoiled, it would need a support or stand such as was used for the famous silver trumpets of the old Bible story, for it is nine feet from tip to bell. But today war signals are given by the army bugle. Now the trumpet, instead of just calling to battle, is really a singing horn. Yet, even when heard with other instruments, its proud, ringing voice helps make music to inspire hearers to brave and noble deeds.

WHAT IS THE DIFFERENCE BETWEEN A TRUMPET AND A TROMBONE?

The Italians sometimes call the trombone the *Tromba Spezzata* or the "broken trumpet," because its tube is shortened by sliding one half over the other instead of using valves. They have another name for it, meaning "big trumpet." These are good names, for, if the trumpet and the trombone were uncoiled and placed side by side, they would be alike in shape and length; but, being larger around, the trombone has a deeper voice.

WHAT IS THE FRENCH HORN LIKE?

The old-time hunting horn is now the French horn. It has a sweet, wistful voice. The name and the gentle voice came after a musician used it in his orchestra to remind his audience that his music was about a hunting party. No horn had ever before been used in a concert hall. In those days only stringed instruments were used in orchestras. Because this happened in France, the horn was ever after called the French horn. The people liked the idea of the hunting call in the music, but they thought the tones of the horn too loud and harsh. It had to be made more mellow. In doing this they made the tube longer and more flaring. Its 15-foot length is still coiled in a circle as in its old hunting days, but it is no longer carried over the head of the player. Now its voice is haunting and faraway; it is a dreamer recalling mysterious woodland haunts of long, long ago.

The cornet is the good sport of the high school orchestra. If there is no trumpet, it will take the trumpet's part and do it very well. It often has to do this because it is more easily played. In shape, the cornet is between a horn and a trumpet. Its voice is not as brilliant as that of the trumpet, because the tube of the cornet is more flaring. In the school band and every other brass band, the cornet is very important. It always plays the melody.

44

The tuba is a bass singer. If it were uncoiled and standing on its big flaring bell, a man on the top of a 12-foot ladder could barely reach the mouthpiece. It is the largest and the longest of all brass instruments and sounds the deepest tone. Yet, for all its size, the tuba's big voice can sing smoothly and gently. It can play a very sprightly tune, too. When it does, it is not, as one might imagine, like a dancing elephant, but more like a very agile clown.

The sousaphone is another large tuba, which is named after Sousa, the bandmaster who composed "The Stars and Stripes Forever." Its great flaring tube is circled so that it can be slipped over the head and rested on the shoulder of the player. In this way it is easily carried in marching bands. The deep-voiced recording bass is in the tuba group. Its tube is coiled like that of the other tuba. The recording bass has its bell tipped slightly forward.

The saxhorns of the school band are of different sizes. They are named for a Belgian, Adolphe Sax, who invented many kinds of musical instruments. He made over the old-time bugles into horns, which he fitted with keys so skillfully arranged that the saxhorns can sound even more tones than the human voice. He also invented the saxophone, which has the tube of a horn but the mouthpiece of a clarinet and belongs to the wood-wind instruments.

What great changes and inventions and improvements have been made since that first signal horn! Now all the brass instruments that developed from it can sing as well as shout. Their tones are beautiful, and yet they still have that old-time command.

Fire-Brand
Makes a Signal Horn

A Story of the First Horn

FIRE-BRAND lived in times long past when there were no fences and no boundaries to tell who owned which piece of land. There were only the forests, where Fire-Brand lived, and the great, wide, open spaces.

Fire-Brand, though only a boy, was tall and strong. He could run fast and could throw a stone so straight it never missed the hungry bear that frightened the tribe children.

One day, while the men of the forest were away on a hunt, strange men from the hills came into the forest. They were after the stone tools of the forest tribe. And they wanted to carry away the forest children to be their slaves.

The women cried out at these cruel, wild men, but the forest men were too far away to hear. Fire-Brand called the other tribe boys to help him drive the robbers away. The boys threw big stones at the robbers, and the frightened women joined in the defense of the camp.

At last the fierce men of the hills were driven away. But they took the forest chief's stone ax and the warm animal-skin clothing.

When the forest men heard the story, they were afraid the robbers would come again. So they gathered a great pile of stones and broke off strong branches to be used as clubs. For many days they hunted near the camp so they could hear if the women cried out for help. But after a while the hunting became poor, and the tribesmen knew they must go farther away to find food.

46

On the morning they left, the chief asked Fire-Brand to take care of the women and children. So Fire-Brand sat on guard beside the pile of stones. His mother brought him water in the hollow horn of a wild ox.

Fire-Brand drank the water and then laid the horn beside him. A big stone rolled down from the pile and broke off the tip of the horn. Sadly, Fire-Brand picked up his broken drinking horn. There were plenty of goat horns about the camp, but this horn was a smooth, long one. He had polished it inside and out with sand and pebbles.

He turned the horn in his hands, trying to think of a way to mend it. Could he plug up the hole? He forced a small round stone into the broken tip. But the water had softened the horn. The broken tip spread, and the pebble fell out.

Some of the broken bits of horn stuck to the inside, and Fire-Brand put the horn to his lips to blow them away. When he blew, there came a call — very faint, just a strange little sound. It seemed to say, "Blow harder! You may hear more." Again he put his lips to the horn, pressing them against the tip.

While Fire-Brand had been working with the broken horn, robbers had crept into the forest. This time they came armed with clubs.

Just as the women cried "Robbers!" Fire-Brand blew very hard into the hollow horn. The strange call echoed through the forest. The robbers stopped, fearfully. Away in the deep woods the tribesmen heard the sound. Fire-Brand leaped upon the pile of stones and blew again, still harder.

"B-L-A-R-E! Beware!"

The robbers thought Fire-Brand was some new sort of man, with a voice like that of a jungle lion. They turned and ran away.

When the forest men got back to the camp, they gathered about Fire-Brand. Again and again they asked him to blow into the broken drinking horn. They believed there was a spirit in the horn and were glad when Fire-Brand could make the horn-spirit speak. They called him Fire-Brand-the-Blower. But Fire-Brand-the-Blower knew that the horn-spirit spoke only when he fitted his lips to the horn in a certain way and blew into its long, smooth tube.

In the days since that first horn, many men have worked to make better and better horns. Like Fire-Brand, they first used only horns of animals. And this explains the name *horn*.

FOUR

From Pipe to Pipe Organ

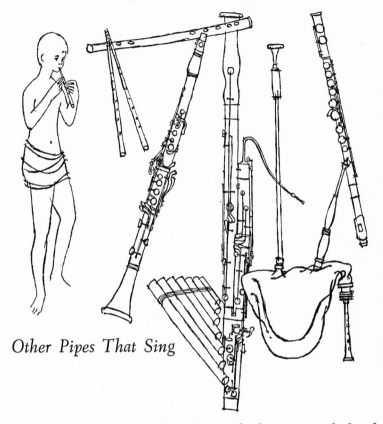

Other Pipes That Sing

IN the long-ago days of the saber-toothed tiger, people lived in natural caves. Although they had not learned to build houses, they had learned to use fire. And they burned logs to keep old Sabertooth away from their cave door.

Now, centuries later, in the caves and in the charred logs, archaeologists have found crude tools made of bone or stone. Among the oldest relics of mankind is a little whistle made from a hollow bone. It was found in an ancient cave-dwelling in France. For thousands of years it had been buried with some little flint knives such as man used before he learned to work with metals. A little bone flute with three finger holes was found in another cave. The tribe boy who made this early flute must have had a few crude tools. He had discovered how finger holes would help his flute to sound more tones.

WHAT EARLY PEOPLE HAD FLUTES?

There are flute myths and stories from every age and from every country. The children of ancient Egypt believed that the flute was given to them by a god, whose symbol was the great river Nile. This was because their early flutes were made of river reeds, or rushes.

In those days the people of Egypt painted pictures on the walls of their tombs. One wall has a picture showing seven musicians, each playing a flute as long as a man's arm. Two flutes made from slender reeds were found in a tomb of one of the huge pyramids.

The Hindu children of India are taught that one of their gods invented the flute for them. The Chinese have no story old enough to tell who first made their soft-toned flute from a bamboo stalk. The old myth of Pan and his pipes is told in many school readers. Almost every child knows how this god, who never grew up, bound river reeds together and made a set of singing pipes.

America, too, has its flute story. Long before Columbus

crossed the Atlantic, an Indian boy had found how to make a flute. He used it in wooing his Indian sweetheart. Each Indian lover made up his own particular love call.

FROM WHAT COUNTRY HAVE THE BEST FLUTE STORIES COME?

But the best stories come from the ancient land of Greece. There the flute was played in almost every home. A gentleman was disgraced if he could not play it. It was used in all public events, too. Some of the Greek flutes were made in pairs. Athletic races and boxing matches were accompanied by flute players. The ships of Greece had trained flute players to mark the time for the rowers. There were many flute-playing contests among the different cities. The people of Thebes, an ancient city of Greece, set up a statue bearing this inscription: "Greece has declared that Thebes wins the prize upon the flute." The story is told that in one contest a player blew himself to death trying to win the prize.

In ancient Rome a flute player wore a bright yellow dress and green or blue slippers embroidered in silver. One of the great Roman orators always kept a flute player standing behind him to sound a low tone in case he pitched his voice too high. Once the flute players of a Roman city became offended and "called a strike." They "walked out" at the time of a big festival and all went to another town. But the festival could not go on without the flute players. They were brought back, given all they had asked for, and in addition were granted three days' vacation every year.

In Greek stories all slender, singing, hollow reeds and pipes were called flutes. There were long flutes and short flutes. Some were played from the end and some from the side. Also there were double flutes. Some of these were joined in one mouthpiece. There were different kinds of mouthpieces. Some had a notch cut in the end over which the player brew his breath to make the sound; some had a round hole in the side near the tip-end over which the breath of the player was blown; some had a little thin piece, or slip, of reed fastened in the tip against which the player blew, as boys today blow through a blade of grass held tightly between their thumbs. The different kinds of pipes and mouthpieces made different kinds of tones.

WHY ARE THESE INSTRUMENTS CALLED WOOD WINDS?

Long before written history, man had learned how to use finger holes in his singing pipes as he used them in his signal horns. Perhaps he learned how to play a little pipe tune even before he learned to make his first horn call. However this may be, it was from his simple singing reeds and pipes that man developed the different kinds of wood-wind instruments in use today. Each one has its own particular kind of mouthpiece and its own peculiar voice. Yet the wood-wind instruments all sing of the out-of-doors, of whispering trees, of trilling birds, and of murmuring waters. Perhaps this is because they were first made by country

52

people who played their pipes as a pleasant pastime and were made happier by their music.

But this is not the reason they were called wood-wind instruments. The name was given to them because at one time they were all made of wood. Now, although they are also made of metal, the old name still clings to them, and it does describe their voices.

The silver flute of today is the pipe with the mouthpiece in which the breath of the player is blown across the opening instead of into the pipe. Blowing the breath across the open end of an empty bottle will show how the sound of the flute is produced.

HOW WAS THE FLUTE IMPROVED?

Many men worked through many centuries to improve the flute, yet when it was played with other instruments its tones were never quite exact. Finally, about a hundred years ago, a Bavarian by the name of Boehm (bām) made one so nearly perfect that it became a model. When Boehm was only a boy he began to work with his flute. By the time he was 14 years old he had made one with four finger holes. From that time on he was always trying to make a better one. At last, when he was 57 years old, he was awarded a gold medal for having made the best flute shown at a great exhibition held in London. In making the award, the judge said, "One person brings a flute with a fine note E, another with some other fine note, but what we want is a flute with all the notes equally fine, and this we find in the Boehm flute." But what years of work had been necessary to produce it!

In carrying out one of his experiments Boehm had changed or remade his flute three hundred times. He had made both the tube and the mouthpiece better, but his best work was done in improving the finger holes and the keys with which they are covered.

The silver flute is the showy, fancy singer of the wood-wind group. It can play a high, clear melody and add trills and frills to rival any canary bird. It can sing a low, quiet melody such as the Indian lover played to call his Indian sweetheart.

The little brother of the flute, the piccolo, is just half as big as the flute and its voice is so shrill that it is called the "imp of the orchestra." In "The Storm" music of the *William Tell Overture* the piccolo represents the shrieking wind and the falling hail and rain.

HOW IS THE OBOE DIFFERENT?

The oboe is the sweet singer of the wood winds. It does no fancy turns such as are done by the flute. Its voice is so simple and friendly, it might represent a young shepherdess singing to her flocks as she leads them through a sunny meadow. Sometimes the oboe plays a happy little dance tune. Then its voice is jolly. The young shepherdess is in a group of girls and boys doing an old-time folk dance in which everybody swings everybody else.

Some people say that the oboe sings through its nose. Its voice does have a sort of nasal twang which musicians describe as "reedy." This is because its mouthpiece is made of two little slips of reed or cane fastened into a small metal tube that fits into the tip end of the oboe. The player blows through these two reeds. They vibrate together and give the oboe a very unusual voice.

Everybody loves the oboe and its deeper-voiced sister, the English horn, which is not a horn at all. It is a larger oboe, which, it is said, has developed from an old-time English shepherd's pipe. Its voice is so tender and dreamy that even when it plays a shepherd's dance there is something about its voice that makes one remember the lonely life of a mountain herdsman. In the music of the *William Tell Overture* the song of the shepherd in "The Calm" is played by the English horn.

WHAT GIVES THE CLARINET A DIFFERENT TONE?

A pipe with still another kind of mouthpiece developed into the clarinet. It has one reed, or slip of cane, fitted into the chisel-shaped tip of the tube. In blowing, the player presses this against the lip. The vibration of the lip and the reed, and the breath in the tube, all combine to give another kind of wood-wind voice. In bands the clarinets play the parts that in orchestras are played by the violins. Because its voice blends so well with other instruments the clarinet is very useful. A large band may have as many as twenty clarinets.

Both the alto and bass clarinets look like giant smoking pipes. The tube curves upward near the bell end, and the tip end is bent in toward the player. All clarinets, however, have the same chisel-shaped mouthpiece with one flat piece of reed, and all have the same kind of voice.

The funny member of the wood-wind group is the bassoon. It might be called the instrument joker because its deep-toned voice is as sprightly as any tumbling clown. In the troll music of "In the Hall of the Mountain King," it leads the dancing imps. In the "Overture" from *A Midsummer Night's Dream,* a bassoon brays for the donkey and leads the clown march of the "six hard men of Athens." But in the "Nocturne" ("Night Song") of this same composition its voice is dignified and beautiful.

The bassoon is really a bass oboe, for it has the same mouthpiece. It is an odd-looking instrument with a wooden pipe or tube about eight feet long. This is doubled or folded back upon itself to bring the finger holes within reach of the player, who holds the bassoon diagonally with the aid of a strap and blows into a long, slender tube, which is needed to bring the mouthpiece within reach.

WHAT OTHER BLOWERS ARE THERE?

Besides wood winds, there are many other Blowers. There are the accordion, the concertina, and the little reed organ. These all have sets of little metal tongues or reeds that make music when struck by air blown from a bellows. The harmonica, or mouth organ, has the same kind of little metal reeds, which are made to sound by the breath of the player.

The bagpipe is a very old and famous Blower. Scotland

may claim its "skirling" voice, but "the pipes" were "calling" in other lands long before Scottish chiefs used them to signal a clan gathering. However, the bagpipe is built on a "Scotch" plan, three or four pipes being made to sound when only one is blown. The pipes are fitted into a leather bag in such a way that all the others also sound when the player blows the singing pipe. These extra pipes are called the "drones" because they drone along in a lower tone than the melody pipe. The instrument has had many different names. Every civilized nation since history began has known the "sackpipe," or *Dudelsack,* as the Germans call it. But for hundreds of years it has been Scotland's favorite, and now whenever its shrill voice is heard, the Highland plaid and bonnet are sure to be close at hand.

The great cathedral organ, the grandest of all instruments, is the aristocrat of the Blowers. Yet this most magnificent of all music makers had its humble beginnings in Pan's pipes and the droning *Dudelsack.* The first organ was a set of pipes placed in a "wind chest" or box in such a way that air forced into the box would sound each pipe.

One of the most interesting of all music stories would show how, step by step and through hundreds of years, this primitive instrument grew up into the splendid organ of to-day. Such a story would have many funny chapters and many strange pictures, for organs, as they grew larger, were often built, blown, and played in very quaint ways. In old organs the wind chest had to be filled by bellows. If the bellows-blower went to sleep the music would come to a sudden stop. A cartoon almost 800 years old shows four bellows boys who have been loafing on the job. The organist is telling them just how he feels about it.

57

An organ that was built in Jerusalem 1,500 years ago is described as having 12 brass pipes and a wind chest made of two elephant skins that needed 15 bellows to fill it. The old story also said this organ could be heard at the Mount of Olives, which is a mile from Jerusalem.

HOW WERE THE FIRST ORGANS PLAYED?

In the first organs the player used his hand to open or close the pipes as they were needed. There were many inventions between that time and the time when keys were used to open and close pipes. When the organ keys were first used they were so large that the organist had to strike them with his fist.

Today the organist, with his hands, plays three or four keyboards called *manuals*. At the same time he plays the pedal keyboard with his feet. The wind is furnished by electric power. With a set of stops, the organist can instantly change the organ tone from the wistful call of a single flute to the grand peal of a thousand deep-toned pipes.

From willow whistle to cathedral organ is a beautiful music story. Every page reveals that whether whistling reed or mighty organ, singing pipes have always been made for the pleasure, contentment, and inspiration of man.

FIVE

From Bowstring to Violin

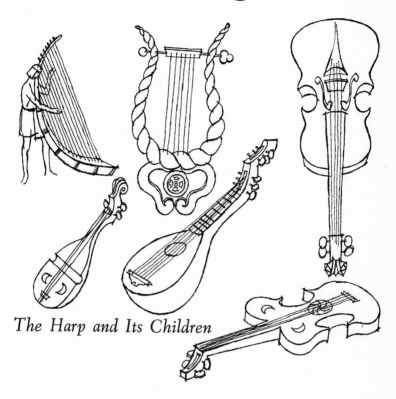

The Harp and Its Children

SIXTY-FIVE thousand dollars for a handful of wood! But *this* handful of wood is a magic violin. It has a magic story, too.

WHAT WAS THE BEGINNING OF STRINGED INSTRUMENTS?

The story begins in the days when the hunter's bow was a part of every man's equipment. He depended upon it for his food, his clothing, and his protection from lurking foe or stalking beast.

The hunter of those times had to be sure of his bowstring. A good string on a well-bent bow always hummed as it sent the arrow flying. The hunter learned to listen for this humming sound. He noticed that long bowstrings twanged with a deeper tone than the shorter strings. He liked the sound of the short and long strings humming together.

Perhaps at night about the campfire these old-time hunters twanged the bowstrings with their fingers, just for the sake of hearing them hum. Perhaps as they sat there they made a little song to go with the humming sound. In some way the bowstrings must have been used for pleasure as well as for protection, because somewhere in those forgotten times man began to make music from stretched strings. He had learned to make drums to help with his dances. He had learned to make pipes that would sing to him when he was lonely, and help him keep his flocks from straying. Now he was to learn to sing with the strings, and afterward to find new ways to make them sing for him.

WHAT DID MAN HAVE TO LEARN ABOUT STRINGS?

There was a long, long time, thousands of years, from the first singing strings to the magic violin. Before such an instrument could be made, man had to learn many secrets about singing strings. How could one string produce tones of different pitch? How could several strings be tuned to sound in harmony? How could the tones be made stronger? How could strings be made to play the melodies of his songs?

60

These were puzzles that man was to work out. While doing so, he discovered that strings can sound in many different ways. He made many kinds of stringed instruments. Some were Pickers, and some were Scrapers. The Pickers must have been made before the Scrapers because they were more simply constructed.

The harp was the first Picker. It probably began when one of those early hunters, in the arch of his bow, put a short string back of his long string. He had ruined his bow for hunting and for fighting, but he had made the first harp.

It would be interesting to know what tones those first two harp strings sounded! If the shorter string was exactly half as long as the first string, and was exactly the same size and kind, and if the hunter stretched it just as tightly, it would sound one octave higher than the first string. Very early in his experiments with strings man must have worked out many such puzzles. Long before written history he had found how to make strings sound certain tones.

WHAT DO ANCIENT RUINS TELL US ABOUT HARPS?

Just as cave dwellings tell of the first flutes, so ruins of ancient cities tell of the first harps. Not long ago explorers discovered a buried city of ancient Babylonia. Among the ruins was a slab of stone ornamented with carvings representing musicians, one of whom is seated and playing a harp with eleven strings. When this stone picture was made more than 4,000 years ago, man had already learned to tune strings. He had a way of stretching them with varying tightness, for in this way strings produce tones of different pitch. All this can be certain from the picture, although it can never be known what melodies the strings sounded.

The tombs and ruins of ancient Egypt are picture galleries of the past that tell fascinating stories about music. More than 4,000 years ago, the Egyptians decorated walls and columns of their great buildings with pictures and sculptures and sacred writing. Because of the dry atmosphere of Egypt, these are still preserved. Even the paintings have not lost their colors.

Processions of singers and dancers and harpists are there on the monuments. Along with these are sign stories that tell of choruses of 1,200 singers, and orchestras of 600 players. Things were done on a large scale in ancient Egypt!

WERE ALL THE HARPS CARRIED?

These pictures show harps more than six feet high. The base, which rests on the floor, is richly decorated. Some are carved with the head of the King, and others with the great lotus flower, which was such a favorite among Egyptians. The base extends upward in a bent bow shape that curves forward at the top. This board also is magnificently adorned with designs done in colors and jewels. Such harps were used in the temples. They show as many as 23 strings.

There are also pictures of smaller harps. Some have three strings and are being played as they are carried, resting upon the shoulder in an almost horizontal position. All the Egyptian harps were without the front pillar, which is so important in harps of the present time. But their form plainly suggests the curve of the old hunting bow.

In all ancient harps, this bow had been very greatly broadened, which proves that 4,000 years ago man had already worked out another of the puzzles. He had found how to make the tones stronger by using a board that vibrated with the strings. Such a device is called a soundboard.

While experimenting with the harp, man made other stringed instruments with different kinds of soundboards. The guitar, with its hollow body to increase the sound, was used in Egypt before the children of Israel made their famous passage through the Red Sea.

There were lutes, too, with still longer finger boards. These had graceful pear-shaped bodies and were hung from the shoulder with ornamental cords or sashes. The long finger boards of lutes and guitars show that man had worked out another of his problems. He had found that, in effect, a string may be instantly shortened by pressing it against the finger board.

There were lyres without a finger board, and with a shallow boxlike soundboard. These lyres were the favorite instruments of the Greek people.

The strings for these instruments were made of tightly twisted silk, or of horsehair, or from the intestines of goats or camels. Such membrane was very skillfully prepared. Man had learned much about making strings in his experimenting since the day of the hunter's bow.

Part of the fascinating mystery about music is how men in widely separated lands made instruments that were so similar. Before their earliest history, the Chinese, the Arabians, and the Hindus all had guitar-like instruments. The ancient Hebrews used a psaltery, a harp, and a lyre. In the very beginning of the Bible story (Genesis iv:21), Jubal is named as "the father of all such as handle the harp and the organ." What kind of harps did Jubal's children handle? The Jewish people left no pictures or sculptures to answer this question.

WHAT STRINGED INSTRUMENT WAS MOST COMMON?

Most of these ancient stringed instruments were Pickers. The early Scrapers were not important and they were not found everywhere as the Pickers were. Until the magic violin was made, the harp was the most important of all stringed instruments. It seems always to have been the most beloved. In Egypt harps were sometimes placed in the tombs of their owners. The children of Israel, when carried away as captives, refused to sound their precious harps in a strange land.

But nowhere has the harp been loved as in Ireland. The figure of a golden harp is woven into the Irish flag. Its strains are woven with threads of gold through the life and songs of the Irish people. There are legends that tell of the harp in Ireland long before St. Patrick set foot on her shores.

However, regardless of legend, the history of the Irish harp begins with the history of the Irish people. A set of laws made 1,500 years ago gives the harper the same rank as the cow-chief, who was an important person in early history. A law in this same ancient code lays a penalty upon one who borrows a harp or "tuning-wood" (harp key) and fails to return it. Evidently harp keys were more important in Ireland than borrowed umbrellas are today!

WHAT IS THE MOST FAMOUS OF IRISH HARPS?

Irish history is made beautiful with tales of its harps. The story of the famous harp of Brian Boru begins in 1014 when, legend relates, its owner, then the ruling monarch of Ireland, was slain in battle. His harp, as well as his jewels, was rescued by his son. It must have been greatly prized, for 200 years later, so the story goes, it was sent as a pledge to Scotland to ransom a famous Irish bard. A song handed down from those times tells how eight years later the Scots refused to restore the harp even for "whole flocks of sheep." In the year 1307 the precious harp was taken to England, where for 200 years it was kept as a treasure in Westminster Abbey. King Henry VIII of England then restored it to the descendants of the first owner. After 250 years more, during which time it changed hands many times and was robbed of its jewels and its silver trimmings, the famous harp was presented to Trinity College, Dublin. There it may now be seen as one of Ireland's most cherished treasures.

Ireland has other famous harps. Many stories tell of kings and queens who played them, of thieves who stole them, of knights who rescued them, of minstrels who sang with them, and of soldiers who carried them thousands of miles into distant lands.

Outside as well as inside Ireland, the harp has a history filled with romance and adventure. Wherever men have gone, they have taken the harp with them. They have improved it greatly since the days of the Irish bards. Of course, even in those times, the harp had already been given a front pillar to strengthen the frame. When this was done or by whom is not known. It already had the three-cornered shape when it was used by the ancient Greeks, and ever since then it has kept this form. The soundboard, or back, and the front pillar rise from the base in a V. At the top they are joined by the gracefully curved neck. The strings are stretched between the neck and the soundboard.

WHAT GREAT IMPROVEMENT WAS MADE IN THE HARP?

The greatest improvement was made about 150 years ago. A piano manufacturer in Paris invented a set of foot pedals by which the player could instantly shorten or lengthen the harp strings, thus making them sound a half step higher or lower. These foot pedals are in the base. They move rods hidden in the front pillar. These rods in turn move little wheels hidden in the neck, to which the strings are fastened. This is very complicated. Only a real genius could have worked it out. Because of his invention, the piano maker of Paris, Sébastien Érard, (a-rahr) became the most famous harp maker of history.

66

The modern harp has 46 or 47 strings. The C strings are colored red, and the F strings are blue. This is to help the harpist, as the black keys on the piano help the pianist.

For hundreds and hundreds of years the harp was the most important stringed instrument. Other Pickers came and went, but the harp remained. The Scrapers seem to have been little used.

About the time Columbus discovered America, many changes were taking place in the world. Books were printed, colleges were founded, schools were opened. Music, too, was changing. More attention was paid to instrumental music. New kinds of songs were being made. The bard no longer furnished the only musical entertainment. Princes in their castles had orchestras and bands. The church had instruments to help the singers. Neighbors and friends met to sing, much as people today meet to play bridge. The practice of singing soprano, alto, tenor, and bass parts together was the newest pastime. Everybody was "doing it." If an alto or bass were missing, that part was taken by an instrument. An instrument also helped choir singers learn their different parts.

WHAT EARLY INSTRUMENT WAS PLAYED WITH A BOW?

Here the Scrapers began to be important. A bowed or rubbed string produced a more singing and prolonged tone than could be made by picking. The stringed instrument of those days that was best suited to this use was called a *rebec*. It was something like the mandolin of today, but was played with a bow. The English called it a "fiddle." The Germans called it a word that meant "jig." Its tones were loud and harsh. An old Spanish poem speaks of the "squalling rebec." Such a voice was good enough for the use of street bands, and for fairs and village dances. Something better must be made for these new ways of using music in the church and in the home.

For many years the best stringed instruments in the world had been made in a small district of northern Italy. It was a land of new ideas, for in those years it was the meeting point of East and West. Travelers from distant places halted there. Merchants and sailors passed that way. Pilgrims and soldiers made it a stopping place. Bards and minstrels sang brave tales. There Italian painters mixed rich colors for their pictures, and there Italian sculptors gave to their marble the grace that was all about them.

WHY WERE THE BEST INSTRUMENTS MADE IN ITALY?

It is not strange that the men of that region took the greatest of pride in their workmanship. The cabinetmakers were expert craftsmen. The instrument makers were artists. They dreamed of bringing a wonderful new music from the strings. Yet they were doers as well as dreamers. They listened to the music brought by travelers from East and West. Ideas that might help were borrowed and passed from workman to workman for testing. Each was striving in friendly competition to make the instrument that would produce finer music than had ever yet been heard.

These workmen believed that the strings with a hollow box for a soundboard held the secret of this unheard music.

68

The best that had yet been made was the clumsy, heavy-toned viol. But no workman was satisfied with it. They made viols of different sizes. They changed the shape of the body. They altered each different part.

HOW DID THE INSTRUMENT MAKERS IMPROVE THE VIOL?

As they worked, the voice of the viol took on a brighter sound. But yet it did not satisfy the workmen. Still they tried to make it better. They changed the curve of the sides. They altered the shape of the top. They arched the front or the back. They used different and thinner woods. They raised the bridge on which the strings rested.

Year after year they never tired of experimenting. The town of Cremona became famous because of its skillful workers. Patiently and happily they tested and tried each pattern.

At last a small, fine, clear-sounding viol was made. The master of the shop and his workmen gave the new viol an endearing name such as they would give to a beautiful child. They called it the violin (little viol).

WHO WAS STRADIVARIUS?

But there was one among the craftsmen, young Antonius Stradivarius (strah-dee-vahr-i-us), who still was unsatisfied. When he drew the bow across the strings of the violin he still bent his ear above the delicate shell of the body, seeming to catch an echo of tones that had not yet been sounded.

69

Year after year the boy worked on in the Cremona shop. He helped to make instruments of the violin family to replace the family of viols. His fingers grew more deft as he helped to make the tenor violin, which is the viola of today. His ears grew keener during the years in which he helped to perfect the violoncello, the bass of the violin family, as it is made today.

The years as they passed seemed to weave a spell for his working. He had a magic sense of touch. His fingers on wood told him just how it should be shaped. Each smallest one of the more than 50 pieces of the violin was shaped according to its own character. His charmed fingers curved and molded soft wood for the front. They rounded and shaped the strong wood for the back. They joined front and back together with sides that fitted as exactly as the halves of a shell that have grown together. Every hidden slip of wood, every least peg, was perfectly made. The varnish, under his brush, welded them together into a violin that at last gave to Stradivarius the magic music of his dreams.

HAS THE SECRET OF THE PERFECT VIOLIN BEEN TOLD?

This is a true tale of magic, for the secret of the perfect Stradivarius violin was known only to its maker. The thin, shell-like little body, less than 14 inches long and weighing less than nine ounces, is so perfectly balanced that it supports the pull of four strings when they are stretched to a tension of 68 pounds. No scale of measurement has been discovered by which instruments of such perfect proportions were constructed. The Stradivarius varnish also seems to have possessed magic, for never since has such a liquid been mixed.

70

Little is known of the life of Stradivarius. As a boy he was apprenticed to a violin master of Cremona. His life story is told in the perfection of his instruments. Other violins made by other Cremona craftsmen bring fabulous prices, but a violin bearing the signature "Antonius Stradivarius" is the almost priceless treasure of the music world.

SIX

From Songs to Symbols

How Music Was Written

WHAT is the most famous ladder in history? It is a ladder that cannot be handled or touched, and yet a little child may move it up or down. It is used every day by old and young, rich and poor, by opera star and whistling newsboy. Yet it has never been seen.

This is not a riddle. The name of this famous ladder is the scale. Its rounds or steps are the different tones used in making music. Each scale tone is a certain distance higher than the one just preceding it. Scale is another word for ladder. Every person who sings or hums or whistles or plays an instrument uses this invisible ladder, because every piece of music is made from a set of tones, or scale.

IS THERE JUST ONE SCALE?

There are different kinds of scales. The *do-re-me* kind with which every schoolboy is familiar shows how scale tones are related to each other. No matter whether *do* is sounded high or low, *re* is always the same distance above it. From the sound of *do, re, mi, fa, sol, la, or ti* the pitch or sound of any of the other six in the set may be found. In this same way the tones of every scale are related to each other. Some scales of olden days had only five tones; others had as many as 20 or 24.

In the thousands and thousands of years man was learning to make music, he used certain tones over and over again. These tones were the ones that his first good horns and pipes had sounded. When he was learning to make the harp, he tuned the strings so they would sound these same tones. He used them in the songs that he sang. He made scales to name the sounds used in music, but for hundreds of years he could find no way to make signs with which he could write what he sang.

73

This is why there will always be mystery about the music of long ago. Ancient people, before they had the alphabet, left sign writing that told *about* music. They left pictures showing musical instruments. But they left no signs or symbols to represent the scales they used, the melodies they sang, or the tunes they played.

What lullaby did the daughter of Pharaoh sing to the baby Moses, whom she found in the cradle of bulrushes? When the boys of Egypt cut flutes from the reeds of the river Nile, what tunes did they play? What was the work-song of the slaves as they heaved the stones of the huge pyramids into place? What melodies did David the shepherd boy use when he sang to King Saul? To what music did the Greek girls toss their bright-colored balls? If the story of Emperor Nero fiddling while Rome burned is true, what tune made him so indifferent to what was happening?

HOW DID THE GREEKS WRITE DOWN THEIR MUSIC?

The answers to these questions are hushed forever, because the people of those days had not discovered a way to write their music. The ancient Hebrews, Chinese, and Arabians wrote music in symbols. But these were interpreted only by their own trained musicians. There are stories that tell how the Greeks wrote music by using letters of the Greek alphabet as signs to sing by. They used other signs to represent tones sounded by their instruments. But although today the poems and stories of Greece are found in many school readers, nobody knows any of the tunes of the Greek people. As time passed, Grecian music was forgotten.

WHAT MUST WRITTEN MUSIC SHOW?

In later days, about the time of the birth of Christ, the Romans also used letters of their alphabet as signs to show how a tune was to be sung. But these letters did not represent music exactly. No one could be certain how a tune written in alphabet letters was intended to sound. For hundreds of years men experimented, trying to find how to make symbols needed to write invisible and constantly moving melodies. They found they must discover how to represent tones, how to show the relation of tones used in the same melody, how to show the time belonging to each tone of a melody, and how to represent pitch. They must discover some way of writing a tune so that everybody looking at the writing would be certain to sing it the same way.

All this time, while the musicians were working, Rome was sending its armies into strange countries to conquer people who were still wild and uncivilized. Later, Rome itself was conquered by savage tribes from northern Europe. Then followed a period of hundreds of years, which is sometimes called the Dark Ages.

The only schools of this period were the church schools or monasteries. Here, with the church, there might be a hospital, a shelter for the poor, and a lodging for travelers. There were kitchens, where many could be fed. There were buildings, where men and boys could learn a trade, and gardens, where food was grown. These monasteries were built in many countries, and they kept education alive in this period of confusion and disorder.

The work of the monastery was all done by men called monks, whose lives were given, without pay, to work for church and people. They cared for the sick of the whole countryside. They looked after the poor. They worked the farm and garden. They did the teaching, too. The monastery had set rules. Each monk had his own duties. From morning prayers before dawn until bedtime, he worked busily.

WHAT PEOPLE WERE MOST INTERESTED IN MUSIC?

At certain hours during the day all work was laid aside. Everybody went into the church for services, which the monks tried to pattern after the service in the great church at Rome, where a few had taken their training. There the singing was done by a splendid choir of men and boys. This choir also chanted prayers and responses. So, out in the monasteries, men were taught to sing the church songs, to march in stately processions, and to chant reverently. Music was their recreation.

The monks found that music helped them in many ways. One very good monk, who was called the Venerable Bede, said, "Music is the most worthy, courteous, pleasant, joyous, and lovely of all knowledge; it makes a man gentlemanly in his demeanor; . . . music encourages us to bear the heaviest afflictions, administers consolation in every difficulty, refreshes the broken spirit, removes headache, and cures crossness and melancholy." When music could do all this, no wonder the monks were willing to teach men to sing.

Usually the monastery had a singing master, or cantor. It was his duty to provide music for the services, train the men and boys of the choir, and make new songs for the service. All church music was made according to set rules, and only the trained choir might sing. In the famous monastery of St. Gall in Switzerland the cantor found that the congregation also wanted to sing. He made hymns in which the untrained voices could join. These hymns were very popular, although one monk said the singing by the congregation was "like the noise of cart wheels rumbling over stones."

Nevertheless, it attracted people to the church and helped them so greatly that even the Pope wanted to improve it. To this day visitors to St. Peter's Church in Rome may see, chained in its place, an old music book written by Pope Gregory nearly 1,400 years ago.

WHAT DID GREGORY DO FOR MUSIC?

Pope Gregory thought if the monks were to be the music teachers they needed more training. He started a school in Rome where the cantors or singing teachers for the monasteries were taught. They studied for nine years. Only the leader could have a book. In those days printing had not been invented and all books had to be written by hand, and there was still no way of writing music so it could be easily read. The monks had to memorize all the songs. In the school in Rome and out in their monasteries, some of the monks were able to compose music. They made beautiful new songs for the service. The monks tried to improve the written symbols for music in order that these new songs might be sent to other monasteries.

WHAT WAS "SINGING APART"?

While they were experimenting, new kinds of music were being made. For many years all songs had been just melodies without tenor or bass parts. The monks began to add bass to the tunes they sang. At first it droned along on just one note as though some sleepy fellow had forgotten to go on from his first tone. But the choir liked the bass idea. Soon cantors were having to train their choirs to sing songs in which three or four melodies were going at the same time. This was called "discanting" or "singing apart." This new way of singing was probably more exciting than it was beautiful. But the choir practiced every day, and never went back to the old way of all singing the same tune.

Another change in the music began when organs were first used in the church service. Now the monks had to write music signs for the organist as well as for the singers.

WHY DID GUIDO WANT NAMES FOR THE NOTES?

Many of the cantors or monk teachers, whose names are forgotten, were very fine musicians. The name Guido (gwee'-do) will be remembered as long as the *do-re-mi* is sung, for it was he who gave these names to the scale tones. It happened in this way: Guido had his troubles. It was not

78

easy to teach the rough men of his choir to sing new songs. Sometimes they did not sing the old ones as well as the good monk wished they would. A story of those days tells that their singing sounded as though they were "quarreling among themselves rather than praising God." Of course, the poor men had no books, and they probably did the best they could to remember how the tunes should go.

HOW DID GUIDO FIND THE NAMES?

Guido kept trying to work out some way by which to help them remember just how each scale tone sounded. He was thinking about this one day as he listened to the men sing the "Hymn to Saint John." The men knew this song and sang it very well. Guido noticed that each line of the hymn (except the last) started on the tone of the scale next above the tone with which the previous line began. There were seven lines to the hymn. There were seven tones to the scale. Here was a grand idea! He would use the first syllable of each line as a name for the scale tone it sounded, except, of course, the last line. But he would give the syllable in the last line to the seventh tone, regardless.

After that, when the men could not get their tones right, Guido had them hum from the well-known hymn the line that began with the tone needed. Soon it was necessary for them to hum only the first syllable to get the correct tone, *do, re, mi, fa, sol, la, or si,* as needed.

The hymn was sung in the Latin language. This is why the scale names are Latin. Here is the "Hymn to Saint John," which gave the scale tones their names: (*Ut* was afterward changed to *Do*. *Si* is made up of *S* for Sancte and *I* for Ioannes — Saint John. It was later changed to *Ti*.)

WHY WAS GUIDO'S PLAN USEFUL?

Guido's plan made it so much easier to teach a new song that it was used by other monks. The Pope heard about it and sent for him to come to Rome and explain it. Legend tells how Guido taught the Pope a new song in one music lesson. The Pope was so delighted he ordered that all cantors of monasteries use Guido's plan. From that day to this, singing teachers have continued to use the *do, re, mi* method of instruction.

Guido has been called the "Father of Music," because he worked out so many helps for both singers and teachers. It is said that he drew the staff lines to show the pitch of the tones.

About this time, instead of the Roman alphabet letters, the signs for tones were queer little black squares or diamond-shaped blocks, which later were called notes. A letter was placed on the staff to show the pitch or key of the scale tones. The clef signs of today grew out of these Roman letters. Clef is the French word for key.

All these new symbols and signs helped. Day after day and year after year the monks in their cells or tiny rooms of the monastery patiently copied by hand the songs for the church service. They found new signs and symbols to represent the new music of the day. They still had great trouble in teaching the choir how to sing in parts. The bass could not keep with the tenor. None of the singers could keep together. The music symbols for whole and half or quarter notes had not yet been invented. There was no way of showing a singer when to hold a tone or when to go on to the next one.

It was about a hundred years after Guido drew the staff that a monk named Franco made notes to show which tones were long and which ones were shorter. He made solid black notes and hollow white notes, some with stems and some without, quite as they are made today. He made rests to show when and how long a singer should be silent.

It was Franco, too, who placed a sign at the beginning of a piece of music to show whether the rhythm moved in three beats or in two. He called the three beats perfect, and used the symbol of a circle instead of the sign ¾, such as is used today. He called music with two beats imperfect. For this sign he broke the circle. Today Franco's broken circle is the mark for common or 4/4 time.

Now, when printed music is so common, these familiar symbols seem simple. They were not simple to those hard-working monks. Monks lived hundreds of miles apart. There was no mail service, no telephone, no way of sending messages except by foot or horseback. Even roadways were few and very poor. The monks could not meet and talk things over, yet they had to work out symbols that they would all understand.

It took years to decide even the little matter of how to make the sign for a sharp. The sign for a flat was used first. It was the Roman letter *b*. The sharp was made by scratching over the sign for the flat. Finally, only these scratches were used; and, as years passed, the scratches were made into the sign used today.

During all those hundreds of years, the monks who made sacred songs to suit the church services, and the minstrel bards who made story songs to suit their listeners, were the only composers of written music. The working people, or folk, also were making music. They made it to suit themselves and did not trouble about rules or about ways of writing it down. Their songs were made just for the fun of singing. Whenever people got together they had games and dances at home. They sang about themselves and about their neighbors. They sang about love-making and about weddings; about planting and harvest. Many of these songs were quickly forgotten. Favorites were remembered and sung over and over.

Such songs are called folk songs because they were

made by untrained singers and were easily learned and sung by working people of any land. The dance and game songs were full of the life and joy of the people. All were very different from the slow-moving, dignified hymns of the church. They were different, too, from the long ballads of the minstrels.

HOW DID THE MONKS USE FOLK TUNES?

Some of these folk tunes were so pleasing that after a time they were borrowed by the monks and used in the church service. Of course, the tunes used in this way had to be made more dignified. The tenor voice would sing the rollicking folk tune, while other voices moved along above and below the melody in a manner that gave a feeling of stateliness and reverence.

The monks were not the only admirers of the folk tunes. At village fairs and country festivals, or wherever crowds of people got together, a rebec or fiddle would strike up a dance tune and a jolly crowd would come together. The lilt and swing of the folk song were catching. Even the "lady of high degree" stopped to listen.

WHO WERE THE TROUBADOURS?

Perhaps this is why noble and knight, who felt themselves above the working people, began to make songs for themselves. Such courtly singers were first called *troubadours* (troo'-ba-doors), from a French word meaning to find or invent, for they invented their own songs. In Germany they were called *minnesingers* (min'-neh-sing-ers), which means singers of love songs. The strange part of the troubadour story is that, after the gentleman had made his song, he either could not or would not sing it himself. Instead, he hired an assistant, or proxy, who could play the lute to sing it for him, even when it was to be sung to the "lady of high degree."

The lady must have liked this sort of secondhand lovemaking, for in the course of time troubadours entirely replaced the bards. These troubadours followed the example of the minstrels in going from place to place with their singing, but they sang songs of romance. From the age of the troubadours comes the *serenade,* or evening song, sung under the window of a lady. The *nocturne,* or night song, and the *aubade,* or morning song, are also a heritage from troubadour days. One of the most beautiful of all star songs, "Oh Thou Sublime Sweet Evening Star," was written in the style of a minnesinger by the great modern composer Wagner (vahg'-ner).

WHAT WERE THE EARLY MUSIC CONTESTS?

These noble singers vied with one another in making new kinds of songs. Contests were held, the prize for the best song being the favor of a fair lady. After a time many a troubadour sang his own songs, and many learned to play their own instruments. Yet these knightly musicians kept their assistants who often filled the roles of singers, players, jugglers, and clowns. With such a variety of entertainment, the singer was sure of a welcome from everyone.

Besides making songs that were different and beautiful, these "singers of chivalry," as they have been called, improved music in other important ways. Their songs were borrowed by the church and gave more grace to its staid formal music. They inspired the common people to make finer songs.

WHO WERE THE MEISTERSINGERS?

The *Meistersingers* (mi'-ster-sing-ers) of Germany were shopkeepers and tradesmen who formed guilds or clubs to study music. Hans Sachs, a cobbler of Nürnberg, was a famous member of this German organization.

Although these songs differed from the dignified music of the church, they were made of the same invisible materials: rhythm, melody, and harmony. Strangely, too, all these old songs fitted into one or the other of three forms that are still used by song writers today. In music the *form* is as important to the composer as a *plan* is to a carpenter, or a model to a maker of automobiles.

Song forms that have come down from these early singers are: the one-part song form in which one simple melody is repeated for each stanza of the text; the two-part in which there are two melodies, one of which is often used as a chorus or refrain; and the three-part in which the music for each stanza is made up of three simple melodies, or of two melodies the first of which is repeated after the second.

WHO FIRST REPRESENTED MUSIC IN WRITING?

While these different types and patterns of songs were being made and sung outside the churches, the monks in the monasteries were working out signs and symbols that would represent music in writing. At last, by the time printing presses began making books, music, too, was ready to be printed. In A. D. 1501 the first music book was printed. In A. D. 1 music had been represented by letters copied by hand; it had taken 1,500 years to make printed music! After all, this was not such a long time, considering all that had to be done. In those 1,500 years man had made not only song symbols, but songs as well. The symbols and the patterns he had worked out were to be used for the songs of all the singers yet to come; the forms or patterns were to be followed by the makers of the world's greatest music.

The Hymn That Keeps on Marching

"Oh Come All Ye Faithful"

THIS IS a mystery song. Nobody knows when, where, or by whom it was first sung. Out of the dim past it marches with the steps of strong men. Its words express reverence. It sings of lives lived in a spirit of devotion. It brings a picture of a monastery choir marching in midnight processional for some long-ago Christ-mass (*Christmas*-service).

Perhaps it comes from those mysterious times that have been

called the Dark Ages. Then, it was a glad day when a new cantor came to a monastery. On foot or on horseback, he had traveled the long, lonely trails from Rome. He brought stories of the great cathedral service. He brought new songs. To the simple boys and men of the monastery choir a new song had all the thrill of today's football fields. To learn to sing it well, they had to work together, as a high school team works to win a game.

In those days music could not be bought or sold. The cantor made most of the songs he taught. He might work an entire year on a single new hymn for the Christmas service.

There are beautiful stories about the monk, Saint Francis of Assisi, who helped the people of the countryside make up little plays about Christmas and the Christ Child. By means of these plays he taught the people to be more gentle and kindly. People came from far and near to a monastery for the Christmas celebra-tion. The favorite service was at midnight on Christmas Eve, when the choir boys and the monks marched, singing, to the chapel for the Christ-mass.

Perhaps some cantor working alone in his bare little room made this marching hymn for his midnight processional. He must have been a friendly, brave young monk — one who had learned from his training in Rome to give the processional maj-esty even in poor surroundings.

Surely, on his journey from Rome to the monastery, he had stopped to visit with people in field or forest. Perhaps he sang for them, and they in turn sang the simple little folk songs they had made up about springtime or birds.

Once at work in his monastery, as the time for the Christ-mass drew near, he wanted to put such joy and beauty into the service that all who heard would remember. Perhaps he put into it some strain he had heard from the folk he had met on his journey. However it may have been, he wrote a special song, full of gladness, yet reverent.

When he taught the new hymn to his choir, the men and boys did their best to sing it beautifully. On a midnight long ago they marched proudly to their lonely church, with the high stars for their only candles. They must have felt the "Good will to men" of the angels' first Christmas hymn.

Surely, some of those who heard the song remembered it and sang it again in their widely scattered homes. Perhaps a visiting monk passed the hymn on to other monasteries. Through the years, the song became known in many places. On and on it marched, singing its way over mountains and plains, until now it has been translated into more than a hundred languages and dialects.

It appeared in a manuscript of music dated about 200 years ago. But long before that it had been sung, with Latin words, as a processional in church services. About a hundred years ago the Latin words were translated into English. Today, in print, this hymn may be under either the Latin title, "Adeste Fideles," or the English title, "Oh Come All Ye Faithful." It may bear the name of Wade — the man who copied the music 200 years ago. Or it may bear the name of Oakeley — the man who translated the Latin words into English. But neither of these men traced the hymn to its beginning. It is quite likely that it was a monastery hymn, for all of them had Latin words.

Whatever its story, each Christmas the grand old hymn marches again:

> Oh come all ye faithful
> Joyful and triumphant.

SEVEN

From Bards to Bands

How Orchestras Are Different

IN THE DAYS of the spear, battle-ax, and long-bow a king might decree war, a chieftain might plan the attack, but a bard led the men into battle. He preceded the soldiers, singing hero songs to stimulate courage, and twirling and tossing his gleaming spear to excite them all. The drum major of today, with his twirling stick, is a descendant of this old-time leader. From the spear-tossing bard to the high school band is a long, long march. It is a procession of makers of music for working folk, for bands have always belonged to the street, the village green, and the public park.

WHO WERE SOME OF THE OLD MUSIC MAKERS?

Imagine watching a sound and color movie of such a long procession. The lights are dimmed. The curtains swing back. The early bards wander across the screen one by one, wrapped in long cloaks and chanting to softly sounding strings. Gleemen of old England and skalds who sing to the daring Vikings appear among them. Then minstrels, at first as lone wanderers but later in twos and threes and then in great companies, pass by. The first minstrels appear in the dull dress of the old bard. As the procession moves on, the cloaks shine with a luster of velvet and silk. They begin to gleam with gold and jewels that were gifts from royal hands. These minstrels in rich robes are seen to move in separate bands, each with its "King of Minstrels." One famous group passes in "gowns of cloth of gold furred with ermine."

As the cloth of gold and ermine group passes, the procession begins to show here and there a clown or an acrobat or a juggler. The music also is changing. The old time hero song is replaced by folk songs. The harp is replaced by bagpipe and fiddle. Mingled with these in the procession is an occasional troubadour with his lute, or a minnesinger with his harp. But mostly such singers would not belong in a procession of music for everyday folk.

90

Little by little the marching bands become less and less impressive in appearance, but no less interesting in this march of time. Groups of vagabond pipers and singers, dancing and begging, juggling and stealing, as was convenient or expedient, pass across the screen. They are pursued by bailiff or sheriff, for by this time being a member of a strolling band was about as respectable as being a gangster is today. Even though musicians were not professional cutthroats, nor "people outside the law," an occasional bad man really belongs in this procession.

But, although social outcasts, they were a merry company. Forbidden by law to play the trumpet and drums, which were reserved for people of rank, they appropriated any tune they heard and sang it with words of their own making. They poked fun at everything from the church to the king, made and broke their own laws, were despised by all, yet were heard with delight by everyone. As the old-time bards had broadcast the news of the day, so these strolling musicians spread abroad the newest tunes. They were welcomed into the homes of the lowly and were furtively brought into the homes of the nobility, for they were the only teachers of the "popular" or people's songs and dances.

WHAT WERE THE MUSICIANS' GUILDS?

Among the fiddlers and singers in this long procession appears occasionally a very important Town Piper, heading

91

the musicians of the town guild. At first, such groups come only from large towns, where tradesmen who enjoy making music are banded together to improve the art. They exclude all the vagabond musicians as low-class noise makers. Then the music of the procession becomes more interesting because, with the passing of the years, more and better instruments had been invented and more and more town bands are organized. Before long, all communities of any size have musicians' guilds or clubs.

WHO WAS THE PIPER-KING?

Strutting along very pompously in the procession every now and then comes the Piper-King. It is his duty to take care that no piper, drummer, fiddler, or player on any instrument be allowed to perform unless properly enrolled as a guild member. The musicians' union is not so modern after all! The Piper-King provides or arranges the music of all festivities. The number of musicians is regulated by the rank of the family giving the festival. A "full band" can only officiate on a civic or state occasion or in a religious festival. An alderman may employ only a selected number of the band players. If a citizen employs more than four to six pipers, both the citizen and the Piper-King have to pay a fine.

These town bands of old have fifes, flutes, oboes, bagpipes, fiddles, viols, and drums. In the course of time the sound of horns and trombones is heard. The procession begins really to march in something like a band formation. Little by little the Piper-King has arranged for music in the church. Impressive bands of horn players, four to six in a group, pass, playing a simple old chorale in beautiful harmony. These are the "town players," appointed to play chorales from the belfry of the town church on Christmas Eve, New Year's Day, and Easter.

WHAT WAS THE "ROYAL NOISE"?

By-and-by, above the dance tunes of strolling fiddles and the sounds of the viols and flutes in the town band, comes the ear-splitting din of trumpets. The early English word for band was "noise." The "Royal Noise" of the court of King Henry VIII (the English Bluebeard and musician king) was composed of 14 trumpets, 10 trombones, four drums, four tambourines, one bagpipe, three rebecs, and two viols! No wonder its name was "noise"! In those years each court had its trumpeter corps. The greater the court, the more trumpeters, and the larger the "noise." These were not bands for the everyday folk; but, when they marched, anyone might hear them.

As the court bands pass, the sound of marching feet changes to the sound of horses' hoofs. The cavalry bands come into view. Trumpets make more interesting music when the meaning of the trumpet call is understood. Each different call had been taught by ear. It was a military band secret that could not be trusted to written notation.

WHAT WAS THE FIRST REGIMENTAL BAND?

As the cavalry passes, a new kind of military band appears. It is the first official regimental band of France, which King Louis XIV has organized under the leadership of Lully (lū-lē′), the greatest musician of his time. The music is different because Lully composed military marches to be played by flutes, oboes, and bassoons, with drums. To be sure, French military bands with trumpets and horns follow in the procession; but these are quite separate from the reed bands. Whether trumpet or reed, these bands from the days of King Louis XIV are splendidly uniformed; for if Louis XIV likes anything better than music, it is gorgeous finery and showy dress.

In watching and hearing such a procession, it is fun to listen for the voice of the clarinet. It was a great day for band music when this instrument was invented. With the French horn to help, the procession of the music of the people now steadily improves.

WHAT WERE OTHER FAMOUS BANDS?

The procession is brightened, too, by the brilliant uniforms of the state bands of different nations. The Coldstream Guards of Scotland, the Prussian Life Guards, the Paris Guards of France, and a dozen others, each preceded by its national standard, pass in splendid review. Finally, among the passing standards, the flag of the United States of America appears. Following it comes the famous Gilmore band represented as it toured Europe in 1878. These fine marchers from the U.S.A. are followed by splendid music from Old World organizations of tradesmen and laborers — factory hands of England in splendid bands playing "Rule Britannia," the "Hallelujah Chorus," Mendelssohn's (men′-del-son) "Wedding March." This is truly music for the masses, made by their fellow workmen.

94

Suddenly from the echoes of the many horns comes a familiar strain. John Philip Sousa and his United States Marine Band playing "The Stars and Stripes Forever" bring every spectator to his feet. This famous bandmaster, the first American musician to receive an English decoration, is wearing the medal of the Victorian Order, which was bestowed upon him by King Edward himself. The appearance of Sousa's famous band, important as it was, would be only an incident in an endless procession that marches on as the curtains swing together and light again floods the auditorium, for as long as man makes music for the people there will be marching bands in splendid pageantry.

There are splendid bands that do not march. These are orchestral bands that play orchestral music. The difference between orchestra and band lies in the importance given to the stringed instruments. Violins and cellos are not good marchers and cannot be included in a marching band. Another reason for the difference is that wind instruments are likely to become unpleasant when played in large numbers indoors. In the past a band was sometimes turned into an orchestra by letting the extra clarinets and trumpets stay at home and filling their places with violins and other members of the string family.

WHEN IS AN ORCHESTRA BETTER THAN A BAND?

Experiments of this kind began to be made about the time colonists were coming to America. When accompaniments for operas came into demand, it was found that an

95

orchestra with a dozen violins furnished a better background for singers than a band with the same number of clarinets and cornets. Little by little during the next hundred years, the distinction between band and orchestra became more clear. A band played open-air music for marching and parades. An orchestra played concert or stage music.

Orchestras are less spectacular than bands; and, until the radio opened the concert halls to everybody, they were also less popular. Now, instead of being heard only in big cities, the finest orchestral concerts of the world are heard in the most remote towns. Since this has come about, people are comparing orchestral and band music. They are interested to learn why and how orchestral music is different from the music of a band.

WHAT INSTRUMENT MADE THE ORCHESTRA POSSIBLE?

The story of the orchestra began when the violin family replaced the viols, because up to that time what had been called orchestras were really only groups of players who accompanied singers. Such groups were usually spoken of as bands. The violin proved to musicians that instrumental music could be as expressive as vocal music.

When they found how to use the voice of the violin, they began to experiment with voices of other instruments. They found that instruments, both alone and in combinations, could be made to represent different kinds and shades of feeling.

Those were the days of great painters. All people, the nobility and the masses, were interested in the masterpieces of their artists. Much attention was being paid to combinations of colors that expressed certain definite feelings. People looked at pictures to find out how the artist grouped his figures to bring about a balance that was satisfying. People understood that the arrangement of lights and shadows in a painting helped the artist to tell his picture-story without the use of words.

HOW DO MUSICIANS USE INSTRUMENTS AND MELODIES?

The makers of music gradually seemed to become aware that music, too, is a language that can speak without words. They began using instruments to express light and shadow, as an artist uses his color tubes. Also, as the artist arranges figures to give his pictures balance, so musicians began to use melodies to balance each other and make music that was satisfying. They worked out certain patterns or forms that became standard. All this took many years.

Musicians experimented with combinations of instruments in connection with the operas, which were then also an experiment in telling a story with music and words and actions. The instrumental players were grouped in a space between audience and stage. This space was called the orchestra. The word, in Greek, means a place in which to dance. Musicians began to use that name for the instruments as a group. They spoke of music for the orchestra as they had been accustomed to speak of music for the church.

HOW WERE THE INSTRUMENTS DIVIDED INTO GROUPS?

In making orchestral music there was much experimenting. The most successful of the early composers was

Haydn (high'dn). He tried using instruments as he might a group of singers. He treated the violin family as a choir. The violins he divided into altos and sopranos. The violas were his tenors and the violoncellos were the basses. For special bass effects Haydn used the big viols. Later on, the wood winds made up another choir, the brasses still another, and all the percussions together made up a fourth group that became known as "the battery." Now, with these four groups of instruments to combine, composers began to consider orchestral music as important as either opera or oratorio.

HOW WERE THE VOICES OF THE INSTRUMENT MADE TO SING?

Listening to the experiments of musicians, the public also began to discover that instrumental music, quite apart from either words or acting, could be very interesting all by itself. There were several reasons for this discovery. All instruments were being improved. The voice of the French horn was becoming soft and beautiful. The flute tones were more true. Valves were working wonders with all the wind instruments. The harp had been given more strings. Its stronger frame permitted the strings to be more tightly stretched. The piano was developing. Best of all, the violin choir was proving to be as expressive as a choir of human voices.

The second important reason why instrumental music of itself was found to be interesting was that schools of music had been established, and men were learning how to combine musical tones in groups called chords. They worked out a science governing the use of chords. Early builders made simple dwelling places and knew nothing of the science of architecture, which later was needed in building great cathedrals. Early artists scratched outlines of animals on rocks, but a masterpiece such as the "Song of the Lark" could come only after centuries of experiments that developed the science of color, form, and composition.

The simple folk tunes had been the natural music of the people, made, as the early shelters and pictures were, without thought of rules or science. The early monks, writing the church service, began the experiments out of which grew the science of harmony. Orchestral music developed as musicians learned more about the laws of this science.

HOW DOES THE MUSIC OF AN ORCHESTRA DIFFER FROM THAT OF A BAND?

Since the marching band cannot use strings, its music is less varied than that made by an orchestra. The rhythm is very important. The tunes, the instruments, and the harmony all emphasize this primitive element or part of music, namely, rhythm. Everybody enjoys band music the first time it is heard. But people must have training to enjoy much orchestral music; people must have opportunity to hear it often. Learning to enjoy orchestral music without hearing it is like learning to swim without water.

WHAT IS "COLOR" IN MUSIC?

Rhythm, tune, and harmony are equally important in orchestral music, but along with these the composer uses color — since the voice of each instrument has its own individual sound. For example, the trumpet is described as having a bright tone color. In addition, every instrument has different shades of tone color. The trumpet tone can be made more brilliant or less bright at the will of the player. This is true of the voice of each instrument. A large orchestra has from 80 to 100 players. Think of all the varying shades of tone color it can produce!

The composer of orchestral music must know how to mix and blend the tones of these instruments. He must depend upon players who are skillful enough to produce just the kind of tone he asks for and at just the instant it is needed in the music. There must be a very broadly trained interpreter, or director, who knows what effect the composer wants and how to help the players produce it. He is the conductor.

Orchestra men must have days and weeks of practice alone and of rehearsal together. The men and the conductor are all experts and receive high salaries. This is why symphony orchestras can be maintained only in large cities.

WHY IS TRAINING IN MUSIC APPRECIATION NECESSARY?

To enjoy orchestral music one must be trained to listen thoughtfully, to remember tunes, to recognize instrument voices, alone and in combinations, and to follow the design or plan upon which the composer builds his "cathedral of sound." School classes, even for lower grades, are training pupils to listen thoughtfully to music. Orchestras of the high school and radio are giving pupils opportunity to hear instruments played skillfully, alone and in combinations. In this way people are learning to listen, to enjoy the masterpieces composed for the orchestra, and to understand the language that speaks without words.

Since the days of Gilmore and Sousa, the word "band" has new meanings — dance band, jazz band, name bands are all quite different. But the splendid high school and college marching bands keep alive the traditional thrills for the masses, whenever and wherever a parade passes along the street.

EIGHT

From Church to Theater

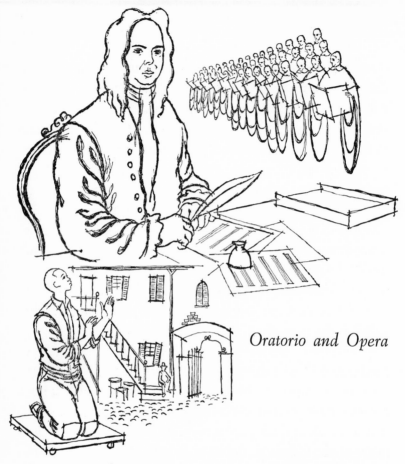

Oratorio and Opera

ORATORIO and opera are names for two different kinds of music stories. They are not told or sung by one person as the old-time bard stories were. Instead, for both oratorio and opera, the story is sung by a large group of people, with a special solo singer to represent each leading character in the story. Oratorio and opera might be called music twins, for both began in Italy in the year 1600 and in those days both were dramatized, or acted out, as well as sung.

WHAT DO THE NAMES MEAN?

Oratorio began in the church. The name comes from a church room where orisons (prayers) were offered. In those days such a room was called the *oratory*. The first music-story dramas were given in the church oratory. The other twin, opera, is named from a Latin word that means *operate* or *work,* because its music had been "worked" over before-hand and was not improvised on the spur of the moment as were many songs.

For 300 years oratorio and opera were everywhere considered the two most important kinds of music that man had made. For a while in Italy these twins grew up close together. Then their ways parted, and each had its own history. Oratorio is the child of the church; opera became the child of the theater.

Fifty years before the first oratorio was produced, the good Father Neri (nā′re), in one of the churches of Rome, was put in charge of the children and youth of the parish. He must have been as wise as he was good, for he understood that all work and no play was dull business. He arranged many of the lessons in the form of little plays, by which he taught the youth to be kind and gentle. Then, knowing how Italian boys loved to sing, he chose the Pope's own choir leader to set parts of the drama to music for boys' voices. At first there were only choruses in which all could join, but later there were solos for the best singers. They represented the characters in the story. But the chorus in which all could sing was the important part.

Another clever idea of the wise priest was to divide the musical play into two acts. The first act was used as a coaxer to bring the people to his service on time. Between the first and the last act, the sermon was given. This was always a talk about the story that was being acted and sung. After this explanation, the last act of the story was performed.

Father Neri knew of some plays that had entirely misused and distorted Bible stories. These were irreverent. Because of this he took great care that the plays he was sponsoring were both reverent and dignified. He dramatized "The Prodigal Son," "The Good Samaritan," and other stories from the Bible. He also dramatized stories from other sources as lessons in moral training for the boys. To make these interesting, he used both costumes and scenery. But he made the music more important than either of these. He seems never to have overlooked the fact that he was educating the young people who had been placed in his care.

For half a hundred years the plays he arranged drew crowds to the chapel. People outside the church began to talk about them. They came to the notice of the poets and the musicians of Rome. Other persons besides Father Neri began to write verses for the plays. The finest musicians of Italy began to set the verses to music.

Five years after Father Neri's death, the first performance to be called an oratorio was given in the oratory of his

104

church, with very grand scenery and gorgeous costumes. In many ways this oratorio was much like its twin, opera, and for many years in Italy, the early home of both, the chief difference was that oratorios always had a sacred story. Both had instrumental music, solos, choruses, and also a new kind of chantlike song for one voice alone. This was called a *recitative* because it recited the story that connected the other songs of the play.

WHAT WERE THE PASSION ORATORIOS?

While oratorios with costume and action were being given in the churches of Italy, musicians of Germany were setting to music the Bible story of the crucifixion, which was sung without costume or action. Such compositions were known as *Passion Music*. Passion oratorios, as they were developed in Germany, were far too sacred to be associated with any stage display. The music itself could interest people and draw them to the church for worship.

The most famous of these Passion oratorios were composed by Johann Sebastian Bach (bahk), who has made the world's most sublime and beautiful sacred music. Bach had grown up a choir boy, and his later life was spent as a singing teacher and as organist and choir director. His love of the strong, sincere choral of the Protestant church is reflected in his *Passion Music*. This, the *Mass in B Minor*, and *Christmas Oratorio*, composed early in the 18th century, have been looked upon as the supreme works of their field; and they are regarded by musicians much as Shakespeare's works are regarded by students of English literature.

In England, at the same time, another kind of oratorio was being sung. Bach had composed his *Passion Music* for church service. In England, Handel, another of the world's great musicians, composed oratorios for concert entertainments. Even though these were Bible stories, they were less serious than the *Passion Music* and were designed to entertain as well as to inspire listeners.

Handel was a German by birth. In his youth he, like Bach, had learned to sing the reverent hymns of the German church. When a young man, he had traveled much. He had heard oratorios in Italy, where at that time more attention was given to letting the singer show off his voice than to making the music express the meaning of the words.

WHAT IS AN ARIA?

Handel's oratorios were more showy than the *Passion Music* of Bach. He used an orchestra that opened the story with an overture of instrumental music. He used many different kinds of songs. A solo for one voice alone, which Handel called an *aria*, might be a simple, sweet song with the voice singing above the soft tones of one instrument. It might be a very dramatic song with many instruments to help emphasize the climax. It might be a happy song in which the voice made trills and turns as though imitating a canary bird. Such a solo, if sung by a soprano voice, might have the flute to help express the feeling of grace and lightness of the aria. Handel's "I Know That My Redeemer Liveth" is an example of an aria.

106

Handel used duets, or songs for two voices, that answered each other, one singing at a time or perhaps both together, making beautiful harmony. He made trios, or songs for three voices, and quartets, or songs for four.

But Handel made the choruses the great feature of his oratorio. After 300 years these are still the marvel of all who sing or hear a Handel oratorio. His masterpiece is *Messiah*. It is one of the best known and loved of all oratorios. The beautiful melodies of its solos are familiar to both young and old. No other oratorio has so many stirring choruses. The music of its "Hallelujah" chorus has proved that sacred music, without costumes, scenery, or action, can be entertaining and worshipful at the same time.

WHAT ARE CANTATAS?

Since the time of Bach and Handel, many famous musicians have composed oratorios and cantatas (little oratorios). Easter and Christmas festivals are made beautiful with such music, and each season it attracts throngs of listeners. Man has made this music, which by itself can draw people to the church service and hold their interest because it has the power to express their deepest religious feelings.

While oratorio was growing and changing, the other twin, opera, had grown and changed, too. From the very beginning opera was planned for entertainment. While Father Neri in Rome was experimenting with Bible stories set to music and action, a group of Italian musicians and writers in the city of Florence, only a short distance away, were experimenting with old Greek stories set to music and action.

It was only a few months after the first oratorio was given in Rome that the first opera was given in Florence. Its subject was a Greek myth. The opera was a part of the festivities for the marriage of the King of France to an Italian princess. It was a grand occasion. Visitors from many courts were present. During the festival the opera created more interest than the bride and groom.

After the festival the interest still continued. In those days Italy was the musical center of the world, and for the next 200 years musicians from all over Europe came there to hear and study opera. An old-time announcement of the Italian opera described it as "an entertainment where intellect and all the noblest sentiments are fascinated at one and the same time by the most delectable art ever devised by human genius." The extravagant notice further pointed out that opera included literature, acting, singing in chorus and solo, instrumental music, dancing, costumes, and scenery. No wonder the world made a path to Italy to see what all the excitement was about!

WHAT WAS ADDED TO OPERA?

The Italians and the musicians who came from other lands kept on with their experiments in this new kind of music. They tried different kinds of stories. They tried all the kinds of songs that were used in oratorio, adding dance songs and comic songs. Unlike the oratorio, the opera chorus was never so important as the solos, and for a time the whole opera seemed to be centered around the solo singers. Each character must have one or two very long and showy arias, no matter how they fitted into the story of the opera.

Although the chorus was neglected, the orchestra came in for its share of experimenting. Larger groups of instruments were used. These were improved greatly, and the players improved, too. New combinations of instruments were tried out. Musicians never tired of working for new ways of making the orchestra help tell the opera story. One important musician of the city of Venice brought fame to himself by trying to represent in orchestral music the rippling of a brook, the roar of wind, and the murmur of the sea. What would he have thought if he could have heard the storm music of the *William Tell* opera! But that came 200 years later, when instruments were still more improved and musicians had learned much more about combining them to produce certain effects.

In the first 250 years of its life, opera passed through many changes. During that time almost all the great musicians composed operas. Each had an opportunity to make his own operas better because of what the composer before him had done.

WHY IS WAGNER KNOWN AS THE MASTER OF OPERA?

Finally came the man who is still known as the "Master of Opera," the German composer, Wagner. He made

109

changes and improvements of which no other opera composer had dreamed. He believed that music has power to express much more than actions or words. He believed that not enough attention had been paid to the opera story. He selected, from the literature of Germany, plots that could furnish him with strong characters and with very dramatic situations. Then he made a little tune to represent each character. As the various characters were associated in the plot, he associated the tunes in his orchestral music. He did this so skillfully that his instrumental music told the opera story almost as plainly as the words and the actions of the characters. He was not satisfied that a singer have a good voice. He must also be a great actor.

These were only a few of the new ideas Wagner used in his opera. He proved his right to the title of "Master of Opera." But instead of opera, he called his compositions music-dramas.

With the operas of Wagner and the oratorios of Bach and Handel, the Italian twins "came of age." The oratorio is the highest form of sacred music, and the opera is the highest form of dramatic music man has made.

One hundred years after Wagner, an American composer, George Gershwin, had more new ideas. Since opera should entertain, Gershwin believed that it should provide contrasts of light and serious situations, of humor and tragedy, each presented in song, dance, and instrumental music. His folk opera of Negro life in Charleston, *Porgy and Bess,* demonstrated his theory.

This opera has repeatedly toured the world's leading cities. Its reception in Italy is typical of all countries visited. In Venice, flowers were showered down upon the stage. In

110

Milan's La Scala Opera House, *Porgy and Bess* played for an entire week. In Rome, it brought Gershwin the highest honor Italy bestows on a foreign composer — membership in the St. Cecilia Academy.

The Triumph of the Oratorio

A Story of the "Messiah"

ABOUT 200 years ago there was deep distress in the Irish city of Dublin. There had been famine, and people were hungry. There had been pestilence, and people were ill. There had been war, and people were injured. Worst of all, a law of the land permitted that any who were in debt could be thrown into jail. The prisons were filled, and charity organizations had no more funds.

At this same time in England, the great composer Handel was in deep distress. Through misunderstandings among his friends, jealousy among his singers, and rivalry among the composers of the time, his operas had failed. He found himself growing old, broken in health, and without funds. But his courage and his spirit did not falter. When a letter came to him from Dublin asking that he give a benefit concert for the needy, he gladly accepted the invitation. He agreed to write an entirely new oratorio for the concert. He knew that Dublin had plenty of people who would pay to hear his music, even though they were careless about helping the needy.

This invitation was a great stimulus to Handel. He forgot his own misfortunes. He decided to tell in songs the story of the coming of the Christ Child to earth. He could find no words better than the words of the Bible. He began with the Old Testament texts that promise the coming of a Messiah to comfort the distressed. As he worked he became inspired. Melodies fitted themselves to the sacred words in a way that led Handel to exclaim to a friend, "I did think I did see all Heaven before me, and the good God himself."

In a month's time the entire oratorio was finished. Handel called it *Messiah*. The people of Dublin were much excited over the visit of the great Handel. They held high hopes of the results of his concert. An advertisement in a "journal" of the times reads: "For the Relief of the Prisoners in the several Gaols, and of the Support of Mercer's Hospital in Stephen's Street, and of the Charitable Infirmary on the Inn's Quay, on Monday, the 12th April, will be performed at the Musick Hall in Fishamble Street, Mr. Handel's New Grand Oratorio, called *Messiah,* in which the gentlemen of the Choirs of both Cathedrals will assist, with some Concertos on the organ by Mr. Handel."

The night before the performance there was a rehearsal of the oratorio to which those who had bought tickets were admitted. The crowd was so great that on the morning of the performance the same journal printed the following notice: "The Stewards of the Charitable Musical Society request the favour of the ladies not to come with hoops this day to the Musick Hall

112

in Fishamble Street. The gentlemen are requested to come without swords."

This was good advertising. By night everyone was talking about the concert. Because hoop skirts and swords were not admitted, a hundred extra seats could be put into the hall, and all were taken.

The concert was a grand musical success. A newspaper of the next day reported, "It took the people by storm."

There were solo parts for leading soprano, alto, tenor, and bass singers. There were duets and quartets. But the great choruses were the grandest parts of the composition. Of all these, the "Hallelujah" chorus was the most wonderful. In it all the singers repeat this exclamation of praise over and over with every possible variation in accent and in melody. This leads up in a grand climax to the text: "For the Lord God Omnipotent reigneth: King of Kings and Lord of Lords!" It was of this chorus that a newspaper of the day reported, "It was allowed by the best judges to be the finest composition of musick ever heard."

The concert was also a grand success for the poor of Dublin. It furnished funds for their relief. It was also a great victory for the composer Handel. The people of England heard of the fame of his new oratorio. He was invited to give it in London, where his last opera had been criticized.

The King and his court attended. This alone would have made the occasion a social success. But the King and the guests of the royal party entirely forgot themselves in the wonder of the music. They followed each number with the greatest attention. When the chorus burst forth with the first great Hallelujah, the King was so moved that he rose to his feet. When the King stands no one remains seated. On the second Hallelujah, as one man the great audience arose, as to this day the audience does whenever the "Hallelujah" chorus is sung.

Into the life of Handel, the *Messiah* brought beautiful harmony. The people who had misunderstood him, the singers who had been troubled by petty jealousies, the rivals who had thought only of criticizing, united in praise of the inspired music. It restored his broken health and fortunes. It encouraged him to compose other sacred oratorios. But of all his compositions the *Messiah* remains the masterpiece. Its music still thrills and inspires people as it did almost 200 hundred years ago.

Although Handel was born in Germany and became a naturalized citizen of England, he now belongs to every land where Christmas is kept. Each year his *Messiah* again tells in song the story of the coming of the Christ Child. It is a Christmas gift of music that never grows old.

NINE

From Past to Present

How Music Lives On and On

WHEREVER a concert or opera is given, wherever people meet to sing or play music together, there among them, though unseen, are "shadow" musicians long since gone and forgotten. When a silver flute sounds, along with it from out of the past a "shadow" shepherd pipes softly. When a player tests the tone of his horn, mysteriously as from some ancient forest a hunting call echoes faintly. The concert-master draws a gleaming bow across the strings, and dimly, as if drifting on the smoke of faraway campfires, there comes a humming of taut bowstrings. Then, as the conductor lifts his baton, keen eyes may all but see the faces of musicians from the distant past who have made possible the music that the orchestra is about to play.

The fluting reeds, the echoing horns, and the singing strings are not the only musical gifts from men of the past. They have also provided the little tunes and the rhythm and melody patterns that have been borrowed and imitated throughout the centuries since man began to make music.

Before Handel could compose *Messiah,* there had to be men whose music he could study. These, in turn, had learned from music such as that sung by the choir boys of Father Neri. Still earlier were the folk who had made up miracle plays and acted them out with singing. Long, long before the miracle plays, there were the great choirs of the Hebrew service in that fabulous temple of King Solomon that is described in the Bible.

Just as it is impossible to say of any time or place, "Here music began," so it is impossible to say of any composer that he created a certain kind of music. This is because every composer makes use of music tools and materials that have been passed down to him by earlier makers of music. Nevertheless, a few great names suggest certain kinds of music.

Master of the Oratorio
GEORGE FREDERIC HANDEL

What a movie the life of Handel would make! Across the screen would flash one grand scene after another. For

116

Handel became the friend of kings and nobles. He traveled from court to court and was everywhere welcomed with royal favor.

Imagine a few of the scenes from such a movie! The first shows the home of Father Handel, who is a barber-surgeon in the German town of Halle (hahl'-uh). The time is around the year 1688. Little George Frederic is toddling about among admiring relatives. He blows his toy whistle and trumpet joyously and beats his drum so rhythmically that Mother Handel says he surely is going to be a musician. At this, Father Handel hastily gathers whistle, drum, and toy trumpet and tosses them out the window. He will have no musicians in his family! George Frederic is to be a lawyer. There must be no more music in the home, and the boy must never go where music will be heard!

HOW DID HANDEL GET HIS START IN MUSIC?

The second scene finds George Frederic at the age of seven. In his night clothes he is tiptoeing to the dimly lighted attic where the clavichord has been hidden. The tinkling sound of clavichord music brings a close-up of a famous painting, "The Boy Handel." This shows the lad, nightcap upon his head, surprised by his family during one of his secret practice hours.

The next scene shows Father Handel preparing to visit a duke whose palace is 40 miles away. Amid the bustle of getting bags into the carriage, young George appears, begging to be taken along. But he might hear music in the palace of the duke! The boy cannot go there! The carriage rolls through the countryside. Suddenly Father Handel discovers his small son panting after it. The carriage stops. The boy is severely scolded, but — happy day! — he is taken along.

Across the silver screen now flashes room after room of the palace, with George Frederic wandering through them at will. Soon he discovers the object of his search, a fine clavichord. Lovely music is now heard. The charmed duke and the frantic father follow the sound and discover the young player. The father is shocked. The duke is entranced. To the boy he gives a handful of coins, and to the father some advice. He says, "Your son is a musical genius. You must see that he is given lessons."

HOW DID HANDEL BEGIN HIS RISE TO FAME?

Ten years more pass. During these years Handel has studied busily. He has learned to play violin, organ, and clavichord, and to compose music. He has even been the director of a cathedral choir. Now he is in Hamburg studying opera, the newest form of music. Upon the movie screen appears the orchestra of the opera company. The men are "tuning up" for a performance. Among the violinists the young Handel is having great fun pretending that he cannot play his part. But all the time his eye is on the harpsichord, whose player is absent. The director is annoyed. Where can the harpsichord player be?

Quietly Handel slips into his vacant seat. His hands run over the keys. Music fills the hall. The orchestra sits spellbound. The director stands amazed. Then, as Handel pauses, the players of the orchestra rise to their feet to do him honor. The director begs him to continue.

Now follow scenes in which the director is seen helping Handel with his first opera. At last comes the night of its performance. It proves a great success. Crowds of elegantly dressed ladies and gentlemen applaud wildly. Orchestra and singers crowd about the happy young composer. Music students clamor for lessons. Publishers request new compositions, and, most exciting of all, visiting royalty from Italy invite Handel to come to that country. Italy! In the year 1706 Italy is the art center of the whole world!

Films showing Handel's life in Italy would be very costly to produce. There would be splendid palaces where Handel played for crowned heads; cathedrals for which he composed sacred music for grand occasions; and concert halls where people thronged to hear the compositions of "the dear Saxon," as the Italian people affectionately called Handel. But between these scenes of grandeur Handel would also be shown alone in his rooms, busily studying the music of Italian composers. For, first of all, he was in Italy to learn.

IN WHAT COUNTRY DID HANDEL DO HIS GREATEST WORK?

After the Italian scenes there would come impressive pictures of Handel as director of music in the greatest court of Germany. But amid all the pomp and splendor, Handel would be shown looking longingly toward London. For his fame had already reached England, and he had been invited to write an opera for the Queen's Theatre.

To England he went and was so kindly received that he fell in love with the people and the country and became a naturalized Englishman. Movies of his English life would need to show the stage where his operas surprised and amazed his audiences. There would be showy music for these scenes to match the extravagant costumes and settings. For Handel never spared expense in staging his operas. Once he wanted to show a tropical garden; and to make it seem realistic he had dozens of live birds flying about the stage while, to an accompaniment of flutes, his heroine sang brilliant flutelike music.

The life of Handel could furnish all the variety needed for a good movie. He was the friend of the poor and humble as well as of the wealthy and powerful. One scene might picture him beside the anvil of a smithy from whom, it is told, he borrowed the tune for his famous composition *The Harmonious Blacksmith*. Another might show him spending the evening in the home of a coal carrier with whom he often spent a musical hour.

There would be a touching scene when, through misunderstandings among his friends, jealousy among the singers of his opera company, and rivalry among the composers of the day, Handel faced failure. Under the strain, his health broke. His friends said, "Poor old Handel!" His rivals said, "Well, he is finished!"

HOW DID HANDEL GAIN NEW FAME?

But then there would quickly follow another scene showing how his courage and his genius met the crisis. He had composed cantatas and oratorios for church service. Now he would compose them for the theater! He would amaze the people with his music instead of with stage effects. Instead of magnificent scenery, he would provide magnificent choruses. He would replace showy costumes with brilliant solos.

At first the people were not sure they would like a sacred story sung in a theater. They thought they must have costumes and staging to help tell a music story. But Handel knew how to win the public. He composed instrumental music to be inserted between sections of the oratorio. He called such music a *concerto* (kohn-cher'-toe). The concerto, a secular piece of music that Handel composed for the organ, was not meant to add anything to the interpretation of the oratorio. It merely relaxed the audience and created a lighter atmosphere. He composed magnificent choruses to tell the story of the oratorio. Between choruses he set solos, duets, and trios, which kept the audience breathless, wondering "what next?"

Handel was always a swift worker. In 13 years he composed 13 oratorios. The finest was the *Messiah*.

HOW WERE HIS LAST DAYS SPENT?

In the midst of new triumphs there came tragedy, for Handel lost his eyesight. A scene that made London weep would show the blind old man, still erect and proud, being led to the organ, where he played from memory or by inspiration.

But his strength was failing. A closing scene for Handel's life-movie would show a great funeral procession following his body to its last resting place in the Poet's Corner of Westminster Abbey. In the procession would be the great men of the time and the choirs of the Royal Chapel and of

St. Paul's Cathedral. It would show England paying the highest honor in its power to the adopted son who had given the world its most-loved oratorio music.

Father of German Music
JOHANN SEBASTIAN BACH

If the life story of Johann Sebastian Bach were told in a radio serial, it would keep people tuning in day after day to find out what happened next and to hear the music.

The announcer would say that the serial begins when Sebastian as a 10-year-old orphan goes with his brother Jacob to live in the home of their older brother, Christoph.

Sebastian took music lessons from Christoph, who was the organist in the village church. But Christoph was a stern man and paid more attention to the rules he taught than to the genius of his small brother.

DID BACH HAVE A HAPPY CHILDHOOD?

The first installment of the serial would have a background of beautiful music, against which the narrator would read.

NARRATOR: It is evening in the home of Christoph Bach. At one side of the hearth the wife sits knitting. At the opposite side Jacob and Sebastian study their catechism by the flickering light of the fire. At the clavichord Christoph is playing from a book of manuscript music. (SEBASTIAN *leaves the fireplace and stands behind* CHRISTOPH. *As the music comes to a close he steps forward quickly.*)

SEBASTIAN (*speaking eagerly*): That is beautiful, Christoph! I like that one best of all.

CHRISTOPH (*turning sharply*): To your catechism, Sebastian. You should be studying it, not listening to the music.

SEBASTIAN (*eagerly*): I will learn my lesson tomorrow, Christoph, but now please may I play that music myself?

CHRISTOPH (*impatiently*): You? No, no. You are too young. Go back to your lesson.

SEBASTIAN (*hopefully*): Then tomorrow? May I take the book and play it for myself tomorrow?

CHRISTOPH (*amazed*): What! Take my precious book that cost me months of copying? You know it is always locked behind the grating in the bookcase. You must never so much as touch this book!

FRAU BACH (*speaking kindly*): Come, little Sebastian. Come, Jacob. We will now sing the evening prayer, for it is your bedtime.

(*Voices are heard singing an old hymn. The music fades away and the voice of the* NARRATOR *begins again.*)

NARRATOR: It is midnight. Moonlight coming in through the window shows Jacob asleep, while at a table nearby, Sebastian is busily drawing a music staff in his copy book. Jacob, roused by the scratching pen, starts up.

SEBASTIAN (*quickly*): Hush! Make no sound!

JACOB (*whispering*): What are you about, Brother?

SEBASTIAN (*whispering*): I must have the music! I can pull the book through the grating and copy the notes by the moonlight. Please, Jacob, make me no trouble!

JACOB (*sleepily*): Well, if you must be so silly, that can do no harm.

SEBASTIAN (*softly*): Make no sound. I shall be back in bed when the moon is gone.

NARRATOR: So night after night for six long months little Sebastian worked at copying the tiny black notes that meant so much to him. By day, in the absence of Christoph, he dared play the music he had copied. Then one unhappy day —
(*Background of music*)

CHRISTOPH (*coming into the room*): What is this? You have taken my precious book?

SEBASTIAN (*proudly*): No, Christoph, it is my book. See, I have made a copy! Listen how well I play the music!

CHRISTOPH (*angrily*): You disobeyed me! You deserve to be punished. You stole this music. I shall burn the copy!
(*Sound of rustling paper and heavy steps.*)

SEBASTIAN (*begging*): No, Christoph! No, oh no! (*The fire crackles. A door slams.* SEBASTIAN *sobs; and then the voice of the* NARRATOR *is heard against the background of a Bach "Chorale" softly played.*)

NARRATOR: The copy was gone but in the memory of the boy the melodies lingered on, to come alive again in music that made Johann Sebastian Bach the greatest musical composer of Germany, perhaps of all the world!

WHAT GOOD FORTUNE CAME TO HIM?

The next installment would tell of the choir school where Johann Sebastian earned his board and room by singing, and where he had books of music and an organ on which he might play as much as he wished. It would surely tell of

30-mile tramps that Johann Sebastian used to take to hear a famous organist. There is one special story of the night when, trudging back to school supperless and hungry, he stopped outside an inn to sniff the cooking food. Suddenly, out of the window came two herring heads. They were not a tasty tidbit, but better, thought the boy, than hunger. They proved much better, indeed; for when Johann Sebastian opened them, each head contained a coin. With one coin, he bought his supper. The other coin he saved for a later trip.

Organ music would play an important part in the installment telling of the day when Bach was invited to test the new organ in a nearby town. He was young and inexperienced, but he knew organs. First, he played the instrument as loudly as he could, to prove, as he explained to the committee, that it had good lungs. Then, he played as softly as possible to prove that the lungs could be controlled. Finally, when he had tested every part, he played the music of the service so beautifully that then and there, although he was only 18 years old, the committee offered him the position of church organist.

HOW DID BACH FARE AS A CHURCH ORGANIST?

In those times the church organist was expected to compose music for the service. This the young organist was ready to do. He made beautiful hymns, which the congregation loved to sing because they were like old folk tunes. In some of them he really used old tunes, but he added to this music of the past his own beautiful touch and so created stately chorales that are still favorites today.

One installment of this part of the radio story of Bach's life would be a romance, for there is an old account of how the church committee reproved the young organist for paying too much attention to his young cousin Marie, a singer in the church. In those days such a reproof was serious business. But the romance ended happily when Bach was offered a better position in a nearby town, married his cousin, and lived happily.

WHAT KIND OF MUSIC DID HE COMPOSE?

Within the next 10 years Bach composed some of the world's greatest organ music.

Perhaps the next installment of the serial would be a story from his years as music conductor in the court of a wealthy German prince. The music for this installment would show Bach using folk tunes in a different way. The prince played a flute and was especially interested in instrumental music. In those days instrumental music, excepting organ music in churches, was rarely heard. To show that clavichord music could be interesting, Bach composed sets of different kinds of dances. First, he would have a short prelude or introduction; then would follow in turn a stately old procession, a sprightly gavotte, a dainty minuet, and — for the close — probably a jig, which would make the prince think of a village fair or a carnival scene. Often for such sets of short pieces, which Bach called *suites* (sweets), he used tunes that he had heard in his childhood or perhaps remembered from some visit to a fair. But whether he used old tunes or created new ones in the style of the old folk

126

dances, Bach always gave them a charm that delighted the people of the court.

IN WHAT WAYS DID HE IMPROVE CLAVICHORD MUSIC?

Bach was always finding new ways of making music interesting. He decided that the different parts of his suites might sound better if played in different keys. But this could not be done on the clavichord because of the way in which it was tuned. With great patience and skill Bach worked out an entirely new plan of tuning the instrument. His plan was so successful that it has been called the "greatest invention in music history" and is still used in tuning all pianos.

Bach's suites required quick finger action, but at that time clavichord players used only the three middle fingers. Imagine a three-fingered pianist today! Bach boldly taught the use of the thumb and the little finger. In this way also he gave greater charm to the instrumental music of all keyboard instruments.

For this German prince who employed him, he composed music for violin or flute combined with other stringed instruments. These quartets and concertos, as Bach called them, are still frequently heard on concert programs.

In the radio serial there should also be a story of Bach as music teacher and composer for his family as well as for his prince. The music for this would be little *Preludes,* which he wrote for his children. Children today still practice Bach's *Preludes* in their lessons.

In the midst of this happy music there would come the tragic story of the death of his wife, Maria, while Bach was absent with the prince.

One of the happiest installments of the Bach story would tell of his home life after he became director of music in one of the finest schools of Germany. After the death of Maria, Bach had married a young singer. She helped him with the music education of his motherless children. Now, in the new home in Leipzig, with her own young children added, she helped him make their family musicals famous. In all, Bach had 20 children, everyone of them, as he wrote to a friend, "born musicians." Although the oldest were gone before the youngest were born, the Bach household was always large. Yet there were always extra violins and flutes and even clavichords for chance guests. The students of the school liked to drop in of an evening. With father Bach directing, what music they would make! Such an installment of the radio story would have to be a concert!

Bach must have been a tireless worker. It was while he was director of this school that the greatest of his choral music was written. His students supplied music for four churches, besides music for special events such as large weddings, important funerals, and great civic occasions. All this music Bach had to compose and copy. Yet, it was here, for use at Easter and Christmas, that Bach composed the greatest music ever written for church service.

WAS BACH ALWAYS AS WELL KNOWN AS HE IS TODAY?

It is not strange that with so much copying of music, Bach should lose his eyesight. Like Handel's, his last years were spent in total blindness. But in other ways the lives of Bach and Handel were completely different. At his death, Bach was known to but few people even in his own country. Much of his music had never been published. For many years it lay unnoticed and dusty in the old school at Leipzig. Then, nearly a century later, another musician, Felix Mendelssohn, found the manuscripts of the great master and made them known to the world. Bach has been called the "master of masters" because of his influence upon later composers, including Beethoven and Wagner.

The last installment of a Bach radio serial might come from the present. It might tell of the famous Bach Festival that is held each year at Bethlehem, Pennsylvania. It might include people from all parts of the United States, who come together to hear as well as to sing and to play the compositions of this quiet, unassuming man who took the best from all that had gone before, gave it new value, and passed it on for all the music makers of the future to possess and to enjoy.

Father of the Orchestra

Franz Joseph Haydn

The story of Franz Joseph Haydn (high'dn) begins in the kitchen of a thatched cottage in the old Austrian town of Rohrau (rohr-ow), where he was born in the year 1732. It is evening. Before the fire the father sits playing his harp and singing old folk songs learned from his grandparents. The mother, busy about her kitchen, sings along with him. A clear, sweet, childish voice joins in. The parents smile and nod toward the bench in the corner. There sits little Franz

Joseph, gaily fiddling with two pieces of wood. He is keeping time with his head and his stick-bow, for all the world like the village schoolmaster!

The director from the choir school, seeing Franz Joseph fiddle and hearing him sing, took him in as a pupil and choir boy. In such boarding schools the choir boys had regular studies and, in addition, special music studies. Soon Franz Joseph was learning to play a real violin as well as the harpsichord. Then by accident he learned to play the drum. This is how it happened.

HOW DID HAYDN MAKE HIS FIRST PUBLIC APPEARANCE?

During a festival week the choir marched in a procession every day. But the drummer was unable to march. There was only Franz Joseph to fill in. He was too small to carry the big drum, but the director knew that he would keep the procession marching in time. He showed the boy how to hold the sticks and told him to work it out as best he could. Franz Joseph found an old tub and set to work.

The procession that afternoon must have been very amusing! While a big boy carried the drum on his back, Franz Joseph followed close behind beating in fine style. The crowds in the street laughed, but they cheered louder than they laughed. The director was a stern man, but he too laughed.

For years Franz Joseph was soloist in the choir. He was a good student, but he loved fun and was often caught in mischief. As he grew older and his voice began to change, the director was less inclined to overlook his pranks. One

130

day Franz Joseph cut the pigtail off the wig of the boy sitting in front of him. For this he was turned out of school without a penny!

Franz Joseph now tramped the countryside to find work. By playing at festivals and funerals, he picked up a meager living. He slept in the attic of a poor musician who befriended him. The hardest trial was that he had no clavichord on which to try the music he was always making up. Sometimes he even had no paper to write down his tunes.

Once he wrote a serenade, and to find out how it would sound he coaxed two friends to go with him to try it out. They decided to sing it to the daughter of an actor. But when they sang under her window, it was the father who came to thank them.

"Who wrote that music?" he called.

"I did," boldly answered Haydn. The actor, who was just then busy writing a comic opera, took Haydn into the house and asked him to compose some music for it. The plot called for a storm, but Haydn could not make his music loud enough to seem stormy. He lost his temper and slammed his hands down on the two ends of the keyboard, crying, "The devil take the storm!"

"That's it!" shouted the actor. "Now you've got it!" And he paid the hungry Haydn $55 for the music.

Haydn now rented an attic and an old clavichord and even bought some paper and a few books. The leaky attic seemed like heaven!

In those times there were two words that musicians often used. *Cantata* meant a composition for voices. *Sonata* meant a composition for instruments. There were many cantatas but not so many sonatas, because the instruments of those days were not as good as they now are. Haydn wanted to work out a regular pattern for a sonata. He thought that if musicians had no words to follow, they would like to have the music make a design. He knew that a good design would have to have contrasts and different kinds of tunes arranged to make a pattern. He used some of the old folk tunes he had learned from his father. He made up others that had the same happy lilt as the ones he had tried to play on his stick-fiddle. He worked very busily, and often forgot that he was hungry.

Now came better times. People began to listen to his sonatas. Musicians liked the way his tunes worked into a design. They liked the way he always made them follow his sonata pattern. Wealthy people hired him to compose music for their parties. Pupils came for lessons.

Then one happy day a nobleman of Austria engaged Haydn to direct the music for his grand country home. The castle stood in gardens that were like a fairyland. It had concert halls, a theater, a chapel with a fine choir, and an orchestra with the best of players. What a change for Haydn! No more cold attics. No more tramping about to give lessons. And here were a choir and an orchestra to help him in working out his musical patterns.

IN WHAT OTHER FORMS OF MUSIC DID HAYDN
ACHIEVE SUCCESS?

There was plenty of work. The prince had a concert every day. Haydn trained the choir and composed operas for the garden festivals. Often the prince invited a few friends into his private apartments for a quiet evening. It was for these little gatherings that Haydn made some of his loveliest music. He wrote quartets for two violins, a viola, and a cello. Today these string quartets are as fresh and charming as when they delighted the prince and his guests more than 100 years ago.

But Haydn's best experiments were made with the orchestra. The men were so fond of jolly "Papa Haydn," as they called him, that they would willingly do whatever he suggested. He tried placing the instruments in different groupings, and formed a string choir, which he seated in front of the other players. He found so many ways of improving the orchestra that he is called the "father of the modern orchestra." He composed sonatas for the orchestra. These were called *symphonies*.

WHAT DID HAYDN DO TO MAKE SONATAS MORE POPULAR?

Guests of the prince carried stories of Haydn and his music to other lands. Haydn was invited to England and given the greatest honors a musician could receive. But, even while being entertained, he had to have his fun. He composed a *Surprise Symphony,* in which the slow part starts with gentle music and then a crashing chord makes everyone jump!

"Life is a charming affair," Haydn once said to a friend. He said the same thing many times over in his music. After all these years he is still saying it. For Haydn left the world a matchless gift of charming, happy music.

133

Ludwig Van Beethoven

The story of Ludwig Van Beethoven (loot-vig vahn bay'toh-ven) is the story of a gallant battle. It is the story of a matchless knight doomed to live in disguise and all his life to do daily battle with invisible foes. For his defense, he had an invisible shield and sword.

WHY WAS LUDWIG'S CHILDHOOD AN UNHAPPY ONE?

All this sounds as strange as an old-time fairy tale. But this story is true. The invisible foes were troubles more difficult to conquer than any dragon of fairy lore. The disguise and the invisible shield and sword — but these are a part of the strange story!

The battle began when Ludwig was only a baby in the German town of Bonn, where he was born in the year 1770. His father was a stern, hard man, a musician in the court band. Much of his small salary went for drink. Ludwig's mother was kind and gentle, but she had little with which to make a baby comfortable. It was a poor home.

Ludwig was only four years of age when his father began teaching him to play the piano. "I will make a fortune by training the child to play in public for money," the father thought. Drink made him a severe teacher. Sometimes the lessons were given after he came staggering home from a tavern. He would pull Ludwig out of bed to sit for hours at the piano. A mistake meant a whipping. The child's tears and the mother's entreaties were of no avail.

134

Now the battle was really on. But for the struggle the little knight did have an invisible shield. It was the comforting care of his mother. This helped him against treatment too harsh for a child. He did have an invisible sword. It was his great love for music. This helped him with lessons too difficult for one of his years.

Ludwig learned rapidly. By the time he was 11 years old, three of his compositions had been published. His skill in playing the piano amazed all who heard him. But for some reason, little or no money came from his public concerts.

New troubles began to make life difficult. The harsh treatment from his father and the long hours of study were affecting Ludwig's disposition. At school he was moody, and he kept to himself. He made no friends and never played with the other boys. But in this struggle the shining shield was again his help. An old organist, who had been a friend of Grandfather Beethoven, found what a difficult time the boy was having. He helped him with his studies and taught him to play the organ.

WHY DID HE WISH TO GO TO VIENNA?

Conditions at home were growing worse. His mother was ill. Ludwig must help support the family. At age 13 he left school to earn what he could by playing in the court orchestra. He kept at his studies, and by the time he was 15 he was organist of the court chapel. Every spare moment was spent busily composing. Some of the music he wrote was

135

published. But Ludwig was always wishing that he might have lessons in composition. He dreamed of going to the city of Vienna, where he might study with great teachers and hear great music.

Then one happy day the dream came true. Some friend, perhaps it was the old organist, made it possible for Ludwig to go to Vienna. He set off with high hopes and was soon at work with new teachers. Now it seemed that the shield of friendship was to help him win his battle. But the trouble-dragons were close behind him. He was called back by the illness of his mother. He reached home just as she was dying, but in time to promise her that he would take care of the younger children.

Now came hard years. He had loved his mother greatly. His grief for her, and the care of the home and children, were almost more than he could bear. Instead of study and improvement, he must now be playing wherever he could and teaching in between times. There was little time for composing.

WHO HELPED AND ENCOURAGED THE YOUNG MUSICIAN?

These were not all the troubles he had to battle. Part of them were inside his own mind. He grew irritable and more moody. He was unhappy and frequently fell into despair. Then a kind woman, the mother of two of his pupils, began to take the place of his beloved mother. She saw what a difficult time he was having. She made him feel welcome in her beautiful home and, seeing that Beethoven lacked proper schooling, she arranged for him to share the studies of her own son. Best of all, she understood him in his moody and irritable spells. "These," she said, "are his troubles pressing upon him. We shall see what friendship can do for the boy."

Once more the shield of loving care helped in the battle! His devotion to music again became a gleaming sword. He studied and composed. His playing began to attract the attention of influential people. Life became less difficult. There were happy hours.

At last his brothers were able to care for themselves. His poor, weak father died. Soon a wealthy nobleman offered Beethoven a home in the city of Vienna.

In Vienna at this time music was very popular. People of wealth held concerts in their grand homes. Noblemen and ladies had their favorite musicians, who were discussed just as movie stars are talked of today. With the help of friends Beethoven made his way among them. He became the favorite musician of the city. He also began to gain renown as a fine composer.

HOW DID BEETHOVEN'S MUSIC DIFFER FROM THAT OF OTHER COMPOSERS?

Other composers made music that was interesting and charming. Beethoven made music that brought tears to the eyes. He made of music a language that told of joy or of sorrow, of despair or of gaiety.

But a great sadness was with him in all his successes. He was very self-conscious. He had a knightly spirit and matchless genius, but his appearance was anything but knightly.

His manners, too, were "ugly." The strangest part of Beethoven's story is the way in which he treated his good friends and the way in which they cared for him. He would fly into a rage and call them names, forbid them to speak to him, and abuse them spitefully. But the next day he would suffer remorse because of what he had done. His friends always overlooked his fits of temper. They felt that any person who could compose and play such music should be forgiven for rude actions. Thus, even in his great success, his shield of friendship and his gleaming sword of music were all that kept Beethoven from despair.

WHAT GREAT TRAGEDY CAME TO BEETHOVEN IN THE MIDST OF HIS SUCCESS?

But the greatest dragon of all was near. Beethoven began to lose his hearing. In a letter to a friend he tells of his distress. "I pass my life wretchedly," he wrote. "For two years I have avoided all society because I cannot possibly say to people, 'I am deaf.' If I were in any other profession it would not be so bad, but for a musician it is a frightful position."

But he did not give up. He wrote some of the world's greatest music when he could no longer hear a sound. Always his friends stood by. They held a shining shield of care between him and this great new distress.

But now still other troubles were upon him. His brothers, for whom he had sacrificed so much, began to meddle in his affairs. They borrowed money, found fault, and even sold to publishers some compositions that Ludwig did not want published. A nephew whom he had adopted and whom he loved as in his boyhood he had loved his mother, caused him only sorrow.

At last his health began to fail. He could no longer take the long tramps in the fields that he had loved. But up to the end of his life his knightly spirit did not fail. In his last symphony he composed his great "Ode to Joy." Music such as Beethoven left to the world could never have come from one who lost a battle. He lives on victoriously in music, known and loved throughout the world.

Master of the Music Drama

Richard Wagner

The story of Richard Wagner (vahg'-ner) begins in a theater. His stepfather was an actor and often took Richard with him to rehearsals. The two were great pals, and after the rehearsal they would talk together about the theater and about the different characters. Before Richard was eight years old, he knew as much about the great plays of Shakespeare as children today know about the movies.

WHY DID WAGNER BEGIN THE STUDY OF MUSIC?

When Richard was old enough for school, his favorite studies were history and literature. He liked to read stories of old Greek heroes and old German legends. He used to write plays of his own. Then he began to wish that he could write music to go with his plays. He decided to study music.

Whatever Richard did, he did with all his might. When he took up the study of music, a friend said of him that he "ate and slept" with the music of Beethoven, that he went about the street "humming" the tunes of the Beethoven symphonies.

He did so well with his music study that while still only a young man he was composing operas. But there were long, hard years ahead. In those days it was not easy for an unknown composer to find a publisher for his works or a producer who would present them. Yet Wagner never gave up. For years, while trying his luck in different cities, he did all sorts of musical odd jobs to eke out a poor living. All this time he kept on studying and composing.

WHAT GAVE WAGNER THE IDEA FOR "THE FLYING DUTCHMAN"?

He was about 26 years of age when on a long sea voyage his ship ran into stormy weather. During four long weeks on board the floundering vessel, Wagner often heard the sailors speak about the old story of the "Flying Dutchman." This old German myth tells of a sea captain doomed to sail the ocean year after year in a fearful ship with blood-red sails and a ghostly crew. On and on the poor captain must sail. Only once in seven years can his ship make harbor. His only chance to break the evil spell must come during his few short hours on land. If he can find a girl who will love and trust him, he will become free from the curse.

As Wagner listened to the talk of the sailors, he thought to himself, "What a wonderful play that old story would make!" As he listened to the roar of the wind and the rush of the waves, he thought, "If only I could make music to match that old story!"

The four stormy weeks at sea were not wasted. The memory of them lingered and often brought the story of the Flying Dutchman to his mind. Finally, Wagner put the story of the ill-fated captain into a poem, and later the poem served as the text for his opera *The Flying Dutchman.* In this opera Wagner introduced some new musical ideas. He gave Senta, the girl whose great love for and trust in the Dutchman would redeem him from his fate, a special little tune or musical theme. In the opera, whenever she was thought of or talked about by one of the other characters on stage, or whenever she appeared on the stage, her theme was played by the orchestra.

Later, Wagner made special themes or tunes to represent ideas. For example, in his last *music drama, Parsifal,* Wagner wove many themes into the orchestral music. Some of the ideas and characters that Wagner represented by themes in this music drama were those of the Holy Grail, the Last Supper, the Sacred Spear, the leading character Parsifal, the Motive of Faith, Good Friday, and the Saviour's Cry of Anguish.

In the orchestral music Wagner used these special themes much as characters are used on a stage. In the overture, the themes, without the help of any words, give a preview of what the music drama is to show. This was a new type of opera. It was really a drama in which the musical themes were as important as the characters.

141

As he worked on the poems, music, and staging of his early operas, old German legends and myths that he had read as a boy came to his mind. What music dramas they would make! But the old stories were filled with magic. They had talking dragons, magic swords, magic fire, and beauteous mermaids living in the depth of the great Rhine River. How could such characters be shown? How could such scenery be arranged?

Such difficulties only made Wagner more eager to put them into his dramas. With the aid of music he could tell any story. Where a magic scene could not be shown, he would make magic music to express the idea. He retold the old folk tales in dramatic poems. He made dramatic music to match.

But this was a new kind of music. Although Wagner was dramatizing their own old stories, the German people could not understand this new kind of music. Managers of opera companies would not present his operas. Only a few of the musicians of the time understood. They encouraged Wagner and helped him stage his *music dramas*.

At last the German people, too, began to understand. They began to talk about Wagner and his new kind of opera. Some liked it and others did not. But everybody liked to talk about it. This was good publicity, and crowds flocked to every performance. At last success rewarded Wagner's perseverance.

HOW WAS HIS GREAT DREAM REALIZED?

But this was not enough. Wagner loved to dream dreams and make them come true. He had dreamed of a special opera house where even the scene of the mermaids could be shown. Of course, in movies of today this could be managed. But in those times such a scene had to be left pretty much to the imagination. Now Wagner set about making his dream come true.

This was a great adventure. People in all parts of Europe and even in America subscribed money to help. Wagner himself made the plans and selected the little town of Bayreuth (bi'roit) for the location of the theater. In its building every detail of Wagner's dream was made real. He had come to believe that costumes and scenery were almost as important as music and actors. When at last the building was completed, Wagner had all that his imagination could ask for.

There was a great festival. People from all parts of the world came to look and listen — and to worship. For the theater became a shrine to which music lovers journeyed as on a pilgrimage.

Thus the story of Richard Wagner closes as it began, in a theater. But the beginning was a small boy looking on at a rehearsal. The close was a great artist seeing his own drama, hearing his own music, and watching his own dreams come true.

In the story of "How Man Made Music" Handel, Bach, Haydn, Beethoven, and Wagner are great familiar names. But along with these is an innumerable company of all those who through the ages have helped in the development of music, now so rightly called the Divine Art.

TEN

From Many Lands
to Ours

Borrowed Tunes and Immigrant Songs

A JOLLY little vagabond tune from nobody knows where is now at home in almost every corner of the world. Hundreds of years ago in France it was known as "The Song of Mambron." Today the English sing it, "For he's a jolly good fellow." The Irish sing it, "Me father and mither are Irish." And the Americans sing it, "We won't go home until morning," or any other words that fit the occasion or group.

How did this little tune find its way around the world?

It would have been easier, in the words of an old song, to "Build a fence around Texas" than to corral such a happy, vagabond melody.

For wherever people go, their songs go with them. Since the days of Columbus, every shipload of people coming to the New World has brought its quota of songs. The Pilgrim Fathers "shook the depths of the forest gloom, with their hymns of lofty cheer." Marquette and Joliet on their famous exploration trip down the Mississippi had boatmen who paddled in time to their singing. Negro slaves brought their rhythms and harmonies from Africa. Immigrants from all parts of the globe who came to make their home in the New World brought their songs with them.

Some of these immigrants had few belongings — perhaps they carried only a small bundle. Yet, along with most of them there came little songs from old homelands: something a mother had crooned or a father had sung.

What a concert of music! Melodies of Scandinavian and Slav, of Celt and Latin, of Jew and Gentile, of brown, black, white, and yellow races — all these mingling in the great "melting pot" of America. What a uniting of races and customs and traditions this "melting pot" has brought about! And music, like a golden thread, runs in and through and around it all.

In their new home some of these tunes were borrowed and, like the vagabond tune, were used with new words. "The Star-Spangled Banner" and "America" have such borrowed melodies. "Yankee Doodle" is typically American, for in its tune are blended strains from three different lands.

The folklore of most countries grows slowly through hundreds or even thousands of years. But the United States, although still young, has a wealth of folk songs, richer and more varied than any other country in the world. What a heritage immigrant peoples have given the United States of America!

Songs with Borrowed Tunes

THE STAR-SPANGLED BANNER

During the War of 1812, a young lawyer named Key sailed down Chesapeake Bay to obtain the release of an American prisoner held on board an English warship. Key reached the vessel just as the British began to bombard Fort McHenry. He, too, was detained as a prisoner.

All night from the deck he watched bursting bombs explode over the distant fort. In the flashes of light he could see the American flag still floating. Toward morning the firing ceased. In the darkness, Key had no way of knowing which side had been victorious. When the "dawn's early light" revealed the Stars and Stripes still waving in the breeze, Francis Scott Key wrote the first stanza of the song. Later in the day, after his release from the English warship, he sailed back to Baltimore. It was then that he wrote the other stanzas. For his song Key borrowed an old tune that Englishmen had brought to the colonies. Because it sings of the flag, Key's song was named "The Star-Spangled Banner." It is now the national anthem of the United States of America.

AMERICA

On the Fourth of July, 1832, Boston held a great celebration. An important part of the program was a new song,

"My Country 'Tis of Thee." The words were written by a young student, Samuel Francis Smith. For his song Smith borrowed an old tune that he found in a book of German songs. The tune had been used for the English "God Save the King," for the German "Hail Him with Victory Wreaths," and by the Danes, the Swiss, and other national groups for patriotic songs. It is a perfect tune for group singing. It has the dignity and the spirit needed for a national hymn. Smith's words so fittingly expressed American reverence for freedom, country, and God that the song, written for the Boston celebration, has become the most widely known song of the United States.

Home, Sweet Home

"Home, Sweet Home" has mingled Old World flavor. The words were written by a New Yorker, John Howard Payne, often called "The Homeless Bard of Home," because after the death of his mother — he was 13 years of age — he never had a home of his own. He became a successful actor and wanted to try his luck in Europe. Success did not come easily. Stranded in the gay city of Paris, needing friends and money, he worked on a play that was to be set to music as an opera. One day, so the story goes, he sat in a Paris park, lonely and discouraged, thinking of his boyhood. He put his thoughts into a poem — "There's no place like home"; he forgot his ill luck. Memories of childhood filled his mind. The words for the poem came easily — "Home, Sweet Home"! He found that the poem fitted into the plot of a play he was writing. Later, when the play was made into an opera, Payne's poem was set to an old Sicilian folk tune. The song became the hit of the opera. Soon it was whistled and hummed in every corner of London, where the opera was first performed. Now it is known and loved in almost every corner of the world.

"Merrie England" it was called in the times when Shakespeare wrote his *Hamlet,* and Spenser his *Faerie Queene;* when Sir Walter Raleigh spread his velvet cloak that "Good Queen Bess" might cross the street dry-shod; when Maypoles were set up on village greens and spring was welcomed in with flowers and singing. Historians call this England's "Golden Age." From it many a song came to America in the hearts of men. Some of the songs expressed the English spirit of knightly chivalry, others sang the English love of out-of-door sports. There came, too, hymns expressing the deep religious faith of the dauntless men and women with whom they journeyed to new homes in a new world.

DRINK TO ME ONLY WITH THINE EYES

In London's Westminster Abbey, where England has long buried her famous poets, one tomb is marked only by a simple slab on which are the words, O RARE BEN JONSON. Of all his writings, Jonson, who was a close friend of Shakespeare's, is best known today by the lines of a short poem, "To Celia."

The poem, which begins, "Drink to me only with thine eyes," was set to an old English folk tune that suited it so well that, together, poem and melody make a perfect song of love and chivalry. But the story goes much farther into the past than Ben Jonson's poem and the lovely English girl

148

Celia, for whom it was written. The thoughts and many of the very words of the song are borrowed from a poet of ancient Greece who, many centuries before, had written to some lovely Grecian girl, "Drink to me only with thine eyes, or, if thou wilt, fill the cup with kisses. . . . I sent thee a rosy wreath, not so much honoring thee as bestowing a favor upon the roses . . . If thou wouldst do a kindness to thy lover, send back the roses no longer smelling of themselves only, but also of thee!"

Now probably "Rare Ben Jonson" was merely translating the Grecian poet and bringing him up to date. Perhaps it was just that he was so deeply in love that he took any means at hand to gain the attention of Celia. However it may have been that the words of the ancient poet were put into English verse; however the verse came to be set to the perfect old English tune; however the two came traveling to the United States — the result is one of the rarest of all the adopted songs that have found a place in American songbooks.

DOXOLOGY

The *Doxology* tune must have been brought to America on the *Mayflower,* for it is related that "amid the storms" the Pilgrims sang psalms. Because the *One Hundredth Psalm* was sung to its melody, a favorite tune of the time was known as *Old Hundredth.* For many years before and after the voyage of the Pilgrims, it had been known by this name. Then, about the year 1695, Thomas Ken, a young master in an English boarding school for boys, gave the old favorite a new name. Ken was a poet and a fine fellow, as well as a teacher who knew the power of music. He composed a

Morning and Evening Hymn Service for the boys. To one part of this service he gave a Greek name, *Doxology,* meaning "to speak (or sing) praise." For this part of his service Ken used the tune *Old Hundredth,* for which he had written a four-line poem. The boys liked this *Doxology* so much that Ken had special copies made and tacked a copy above the bed of each boy. It was sung each night and morning. Later, Ken's text made its way to America, and the *Doxology* with its new words became a part of the service of many churches. If a song be rated by the number of times it is sung, this fine old music would score high. It might even be known as "standing music"; for every Sunday, in churches of this and other lands, thousands stand to sing it reverently as Thomas Ken taught his boys to sing it long ago in Old England.

John Peel

In England, hunting is an organized sport, and hunting parties are carried on according to long established rules and traditions. "Riding to hounds," it is called, when a company with horns, horses, and trained dogs gather for the chase.

One hundred years ago in this — the popular sport of his countrymen — John Peel had no peer. He always led the chase and always "took" the quarry. No fox or hare was too clever or too swift for him. He was six feet two inches in height and stood as straight as Robin Hood's arrow. He walked with a powerful stride and he rode as though he were a part of his mount. With John Peel, hunting was so important that everything else could wait — even, alas, when this meant neglect of his business. But he was such a good sportsman that he could number among his friends all with whom he had ever followed the "drag of the fox."

150

The song in honor of John Peel was written by a close friend of the famous hunter. In his later years old John, still a favorite, found himself in need. When he no longer could lead the chase, the young men of the countryside gave a hunt in his honor. They agreed among themselves to round up a fox and then to fall back and let old John take it as in his earlier days. When he did, they gathered around him singing this song. They then presented him with a bounty, which kept him in comfort the rest of his life. In Caldreck near the Troutbeck of the song, Peel's house may still be seen and relatives of the veteran huntsman still live there. So do the descendants of his famous "pack," for the hunting dogs of the district are named Ruby, Ringwood, Ranter, Bellman, and True. The last stanza of the song was added by some friend for the burial service of the aged hunter. In the old cemetery there stands a moss-covered stone inscribed to his memory. It is carved with a hound and a hunter's horn. But a finer monument to his memory is the song that now is sung many miles from Troutbeck by young men who never rode to the hounds nor lifted a "view halloo" at sight of a fox; they sing John Peel in their glee club choruses, with all the fervor of their English cousins who sang it joyously a century ago.

Songs Adopted from Wales

The Welsh have a great store of folk songs that go back to the days before Wales was called Wales. Then England was known as the "Island of the White Cliffs" and the home of strange wild tribesmen. Long, long ago, when this island was conquered by invaders, some of these wild tribespeople escaped and took refuge in the mountains on the west coast. Here they defied the invaders, and for hundreds of years they lived their own life. They held to their own language, their own religion, and their own customs. Living to themselves and keeping to their ancient traditions made them seem so different that the invaders called them "Walas" (foreigners); from this the whole peninsula came to be known as Wales and the people as the Welsh. Many wars were fought before Wales, in the year 1282, finally came under English rule. The sturdy Welsh have kept their independent spirit. Thomas Jefferson and other famous Americans of Welsh ancestry were signers of our Declaration of Independence.

Among the Welsh, songs and stories have always been important. It was in long-ago Wales that the first wandering minstrels or bards traveled from castle to castle. Their stories, repeated in "lays" or song-stories, told of deeds of valor of their countrymen.

It was in the songs of Welsh minstrels that the story of *King Arthur* and the *Knights of His Round Table* was preserved; for the "Valley of Avalon" and "Camelot" were in the country of the "Little Land Behind the Hills." In Wales, at ancient banquets, the little harp was passed from host to guest and went from hand to hand around the table, for to these Welshmen, song was as natural as speech.

MEN OF HARLECH

For more than a thousand years the Tower of Harlech has guarded the rocky coast of western Wales. Harlech, which means "above the boulders," was built as a Roman fort in the sixth century. Its tower furnished a lookout against enemy approach by sea. Later, the fort was rebuilt as a

152

castle with many towers and turrets to guard Merimeth, the ancient capital of Wales. Many desperate battles were waged around this stronghold.

During the War of the Roses, when Harlech castle was taken by the "White Roses" about 1468, the famous march of the men of Harlech was composed and sung. In its martial strains the wild Welsh daring and determination are flung out like a banner! Whatever the original words may have been, their challenge rings down through the centuries in that last cutoff phrase of the tune. These words are now translated "Freedom, God and Right," with the "and" on the shortened or "bitten-off" tone and the added accent thus gained put on the "Right."

Ever since 1468 this song has been a favorite in Wales. It has crossed the ocean with many a dauntless Welsh immigrant and now it is as much at home here as in the great mining and shipping centers of modern Wales. Bands play it. Glee clubs sing it. Georgetown University borrowed the tune for its college song. When "Sons of Georgetown" is sung, every hearer agrees with the boast of the Welshman who declared "The marching music of Wales is superior to that of any other people."

ALL THROUGH THE NIGHT

This is one of the oldest of Welsh melodies. For all its age, it is often pointed out as a perfectly constructed melody. It has simplicity, it is expressive, and it is in perfect balance. The first four-measure phrase ends on its "home" tone or *do*, giving a sense of rest. This is repeated. Then comes a contrasting melody the same length (four measures) as the first phrase and of equal simplicity and tenderness. This leads into a repetition of the first melody, which now becomes the closing phrase.

In Wales this tune has long been known as "Poor Mary Ann," a title not at all fitting the poetic melody, which has had many different sets of words. However, it came to the United States with the title "All Through the Night" and with a story that adds romance to the lovely music. It is said that the famous Welsh minstrel, David Owen, who lived some 200 years ago, had been out for a "nosonlawen" (singing night). Dawn was breaking when at last he wended his way homeward. But the flushing skies, a waking bird, and his beloved harp coaxed for one more song. David seated himself upon a wayside stone (still pointed out by the villagers of Plas-y-Borth) and, singing along with the lark, made up the new words, which he set to the ancient melody. This song has found its way into the hearts of all who love song — as a serenade, as a lullaby, and as just a song for everyone on any occasion when people feel the urge to sing.

Songs Adopted from Scotland

With the first strain of a Scottish song one can "fair smell the heather"! Both text and tune have a flavor all their own, and it is a flavor that everyone enjoys. The poems of Robert Burns with their love of home and kin and country have helped to make the tune popular. Aside from the charm of the verses, the old tunes to which Burns set his poems have characteristics as national as the Scotch dialect. Some of the melodies go back to unknown times. "Auld Lang Syne" has only five different tones in its melody, for it does not use either the fourth (fa) or the seventh (ti) of the present-day scale. It would be interesting to know how, when, and where the "Auld Lang Syne" tune began. There is also the "Scotch snap" that is found in many old tunes. This is a tricky catch in the rhythm, which is brought about by cutting short the strong beat of the melody and adding the time thus gained to the weak beat. This "snap" at its best is heard in "Comin' Thro' the Rye."

However these songs began, they now fill many a page in songbooks far from Bonnie Scotland's banks and braes. They have made its lochs and bens known to thousands who never looked upon its crags or tramped its glens and highlands. Scotland has a song for every important event in its long, exciting history. Its war songs, like the clan thistle, are stern and menacing; its love songs, like the clan bluebell, are tender and endearing; its reels and sword dances are breathtaking and vigorous. But of whatever nature, Scottish songs are favorites among the adopted songs of America.

AULD LANG SYNE

When a company of people sing to express a feeling of good fellowship, one song is sure to be "Auld Lang Syne," which is the Scottish way of saying "for old time's sake." Sung by a large gathering in easy tempo, it breathes the contentment of assured friendship. In a more intimate group and stepped up a bit, it becomes a toast-song for jovial comrades. But when "Auld Lang Syne" is played by bagpipers and in double time, it brings the swirling kilts of Highlanders gaily swinging through the breathless figures of their national dance. The old tune may have begun as a strathspey or reel. The five tones of its melody are all that a bagpipe could play. But this would be no handicap to a thrifty Scot accustomed to making the most of what nature gave him, and along with the craggy, broom-covered hills, the bagpipe was his national inheritance.

"Auld Lang Syne" is one of the many songs of Robert Burns, the "plowboy poet of Scotland." He and a friend once heard an old clansman sing the lines beginning, "Should auld acquaintance be forgot." Burns listened spellbound to the aged singer. Then to his friend he cried, "Light be the turf on the breast of the poet who composed this fragment." Afterward Burns himself added a second and third verse. With this help the song of the old clansman became the world's favorite song of friendship. It was in some such way that Burns preserved many an ancient tune. Speaking of the music to which he set many of his poems he said, "I have collected, begged, borrowed, and stolen all the songs I could meet with." He was doing this during the years of the American Revolution. Since those troubled times many of his borrowed songs have been freely adopted here.

Scots, Wha Hae Wi' Wallace Bled

Every schoolboy knows the story of Robert Bruce, fugitive king of Scotland, and how, inspired by a plucky spider to try again, he turned his luck and saved the kingdom. It was in the battle of Bannockburn that his victory was won. Bruce had taken up a strong position between the Bannock River ("burn") and the towering fortress of Sterling Castle. To reach him, his foes must cross marshy land where Bruce's men had dug hidden pits to entrap the cavalry. When the skilled archers of the enemy had spent themselves, and the mail-clad knights dashed forward, taken unaware, they floundered in the pits helpless before the Highland army.

Then the canniness of Bruce came into play. Amid the confusion of the disordered enemy, from behind a hill marched a fresh Scottish army! It was only the camp hands, drivers, and servants, whom Bruce had formed in marching order to alarm his foes. But the trick worked and secured the independence of Scotland and the throne for Bruce. It was almost 500 years after this victorious day that Burns visited the old battleground. Recalling stories of how Bruce had excited his men to valiant fighting, Burns was inspired to write his fiery battle song. The tune to which Burns fitted his lines was once known by the title "Hei Tutti Taiti," and may have been used in imitation of a trumpet fanfare. But Burns inscribed his song, "Bruce's March to Bannockburn *to its own tune.*"

Whatever the early history of the music, it has long been a fitting companion for the fiery lines of the Scotch poet. Even now, when the world's pressing business is peace, together they can raise the fighting pulse of any man who sings them.

Comin' Thro' the Rye

The name of Burns is always attached to this favorite song, although long before he was born, Scotland had a song that went something like this,

> *"Jeanie is a' weet, poor body,*
> *Jeanie's seldom dry;*
> *She draigl't a' her petticoatie*
> *Comin' thro' the Rye."*

Was it the little Rye River in Ayrshire? There, according to legend, Scotch lads of old waited to help charming lassies cross the slippery steppingstones. Then, in thrifty

Scotch fashion they claimed a fee! Some declare the meeting place was a waving field of rye wet with morning dew. Burns did leave some scribbled lines,

> *"Gin a body kiss a body comin' thro' the grain,*
> *Need a body grudge a body what's a body's ain?"*

River or field, who cares? In either case how many paths must have led to the trysting place! The tune, with its "snap" is of unknown origin. It has the rhythm of a jolly reel, and the words Burns wrote are as lilting as the music. Here in our country the two — words and music — have gone singing along together in all sorts of places: concerts, frontier schools, jukeboxes, even high school dances. In whatever setting, the little song-lassie who "dinna choose to tell" is an extremely popular number in the land by which she was adopted.

Songs Adopted from Ireland

A harp of gold on a field of emerald! Among all flags of all lands where is a similar emblem? Where is another such land, holding to its smiles and songs through years when the country was "a commonwealth of common woe?" Yet Ireland in the darkest hours of its turbulent history with "little left but ashes," kept its harp strings tuned and its love of laughter!

Perhaps the contrasts in character traits of the "Sons of the Auld Sod" have helped give the strange charm felt in Irish songs. These lovable people are such a mixture of fun and tender feeling! They laugh together at their own "bog-trotting, shanty Irish" ways. They boast, in the same breath, of their keening banshees and their Blarney stone, their shamrock and their shillelagh, their Paddys and their Colleens! Irish songs have all this and charming melody besides.

158

More than a thousand years before the birth of Christ the Irish myth-cycle reaches back to the goddess Eire and the god Ir, from whom the island kingdom takes its name. An Egyptian historian, writing of Ireland in 500 B. C., declared, "There is a city whose citizens are most of them harpers." Just what sort of instrument these early harps could have been is not known. But the hand harp that could be carried by minstrels was used in Ireland in very early times, and the famous Irish harps such as the one pictured on the Irish flag have long been the national instrument.

Many a brave story from the pages of Irish history has a harper for its hero. Harpers, heroes, and stories, with the "wee-folk" thrown in, lend their charm to every song adopted from the "Emerald Isle."

The Wearin' o' the Green

Was there ever an Irishman who didn't love to go to afightin'? This song has touched off many a public and private brawl. It once set off a riot in a theater. This was at a time when there had been unusually serious trouble between Ireland and England. Statesmen of both countries were working together to make up for the hardships that had been imposed upon the Irish people by an unwise English ruler. But all Ireland was hungry. The people were impatient. At the most critical time in this crisis, a new play was being introduced in Dublin. The playwright, wanting to appeal to Irish sentiment, rewrote an old street song, giving it explosive ideas and inflammable words. The tenor who sang it gave it all he had and — the fat was in the fire! Sons of Erin shouted and stamped, chins went up, fists clenched, tongues lashed out! But fortunately no "skulls were cracked" (at least not inside the theater). However, the singing of "Wearin' o' the Green" was thereafter declared treasonable. As usual in such cases the song became more popular than ever. The last stanza, suggesting America as a haven for oppressed Irishmen, seems to have been effective. There are now, according to recent statistics, four times as many Irishmen in the United States as in Ireland. Small wonder the "Wearin' o' the Green" is now at home here in America.

EMER'S FAREWELL

The story of Emer, the beautiful Irish girl, may be found in Lady Gregory's *Story of Cuchullain*. Cuchullain, or Cuchullin as he is sometimes called, was an early Irish hero whose exploits have been woven into a whole cycle of songs. These songs have been sung by the Irish bards for centuries.

As the legend goes, Emer was the daughter of Forgal, who lived at Lusk, near the present city of Dublin. She was the only girl in Ireland who could talk to Cuchullain in the ancient language of the poets. Her father did not want her to marry a warrior, and persuaded Cuchullain to go to Scotland. When he returned he found that Emer was prisoner in her father's dwelling. Cuchullain leaped "with the warrior's leap" over the three walls of the fortress, seized Emer, and sprang back into his chariot. Forgal's warriors pursued him; each time they overtook him, Cuchullain stopped and killed a hundred men.

Emer's warrior husband was slain through treachery, and the beautiful girl sang this lament and then fell dead across the body of her husband.

160

The tune Emer is said to have sung for her lament is one of the loveliest of all traditional melodies. It has been used for many different poems, and has also been arranged for instruments.

Songs Adopted from Germany

To the Germany of the past, which someone has called the 'land of song and story," America acknowledges a great music debt. Songs heard here every day and on every occasion have been adopted from the "Fatherland." Germany not only produced great music masters, it also was the homeland of those unnamed and unknown singers who helped to make Germany a rich storehouse of folk music! Slumber songs, dance songs, love songs, nature songs, work songs, war songs, and great religious songs for both the Catholic and the Protestant churches trace back to the Germany of the past.

A MIGHTY FORTRESS

When two great men are joined in the making of one hymn, the result should be a splendid song. This is why "A Mighty Fortress" is one of the grandest hymns ever written. The words are traditionally attributed to the great Jewish "Shepherd King," David. The music is by the famous German reformer, Martin Luther. These words are, in part, from the 46th Psalm.

Luther lived in the stirring times when Columbus discovered the New World — when people everywhere were reaching out to find new and improved ways of living. Luther was a young priest who believed that the church also could make changes for the better. To bring about the changes he thought should take place, he became the head of a group known as the Reformed Church. One of the changes Luther made concerned the music of the church service. In those days, Latin was used in the church songs. The congregation could neither understand what was being sung nor join in the singing.

Luther wanted, besides a trained choir, a means by which all the people could participate in song. He wrote to a friend, "I wish . . . to make German Psalms for the people, that is to say, sacred hymns, so that the word of God may dwell among the people by means of song."

Luther knew the great love the German people had for music. He went about among the working folk and heard their homemade songs and from these selected such melodies as he felt were suited to sacred works taken from the Bible. He also chose some of the more simple and tuneful of the church hymns and translated them from Latin into German. He would play these melodies on his flute, and musicians of the day would write the tunes down and add tenor, bass, and alto parts. In the Reformed Church service these parts were played by instruments, while the people in unison sang the melody.

These songs became known as chorales. How the people loved them! How they sang them! Some of the best chorales were written by Luther himself. The very best was the one for which he used the 46th Psalm. To fit his splendid marching music, Luther arranged the Bible language into rhythmic lines beginning:

> "A mighty fortress is our God
> A bulwark never failing."

162

and closing:

> *"God's truth abideth still*
> *His Kingdom is forever."*

This hymn was first printed in 1529. Within the next few years it was known all over Europe. Those were the days of terrible intolerance: wars were fought in the cause of religion; heads were cut off in the so-called service of God; martyrs were burned at the stake in the name of Christianity. This hymn became a rallying cry for freedom of thought and worship. It was a marching song — a weapon more powerful than sword or dungeon. Best of all, it outlived the dreadful years of persecution. Today it testifies to the sincerity and integrity of the old Germany that gave the world great scientists, great writers, great thinkers, as well as great musicians. It has its page in church hymnals in all parts of the United States.

How Can I Leave Thee

This folk melody is a rare gift from the heart of olden Germany. It is only one of many lovely echoes from the famous province of Thuringia. There, in days of old, noble minnesingers (singers-of-love) went from court to court, singing songs of their own making to please listening lords and ladies. There, in later years, the Meistersingers held their contests in which knight or tradesman might compete in song for even such a prize as the hand of a princess.

Thuringia gave poets as well as singers to Germany. It was the home of Goethe and of Schiller. Here, too, Wagner, the master of music drama, found the stories for his *Tannhauser* and *Parsifal,* and the famous Liszt put the

Thuringian love of beauty into his piano music.

The melody of "Treue Liebe," which is the German title for the song, is an old folk tune. The words are taken from a ballad of the 18th century. It is said to be the world's most widely known love song.

During the trying years of Wagner's life, in addition to making music, he took sides in the troubled political life of Germany. Once when he was on the losing side, his friends, hearing that the musician was about to be arrested and imprisoned, acted quickly to spirit him out of Germany to political safety in Paris. The incident is described by Fitz-Gerald in his *Stories of Famous Songs*. It was the year 1849. Wagner had reached Erfurt and was to be conducted across the French border by two friends. As the three hurried through the night streets to their waiting carriage Wagner stopped suddenly. Voices were singing, "How Can I Leave Thee!" To the horror of his friends, the fugitive musician refused to budge until the last tones died away, then he waited to say wistfully, "What a beautiful song of parting; I wish I had composed it!"

It is because of the inspiration and background of such folk music that German composers through the years became the music masters of the world.

The Crusaders' Hymn

In the Middle Ages great companies of Christian soldiers banded together to journey to Jerusalem and capture that city from the Turks, who had taken possession of it. These men took as their badge the sign of the cross. From French words meaning "to take the cross," comes the word Crusader.

The story of the Crusaders is a bitter tale of the hardships of their 2,000-mile journey to the Holy Land. It is a story of tragic failure and death and also of hard-won victory. As they marched, toilworn, weary, cold, and hungry, the Crusaders sang. The power of the songs must have been great, for it helped them onward. The marching song, "Fairest Lord Jesus," is said to be one of the very tunes they sang.

Songs Adopted from Sweden

The Ole Olsons, John Johnsons, and their sturdy, skillful kin who "made" Wisconsin and Minnesota, brought more than strong arms and thrifty habits to the midwest prairies and forests. Along with model farmsteads and beautiful towns, their songs and their sagas are giving a wonderful Scandinavian flavor to the brew of the great "American Melting-Pot."

Nordic songs vary. Most of them are more in keeping with the "Deep and Dark and Tender" description of the poet, for, in many, a certain wistfulness creeps into the melody as well as the text. It may be they are touched by the somberness of the long winter, when the sun is scarcely seen, when snow blankets everything, and the cold is intense. Yet it is under these conditions that the hardy Scandinavians have developed their world-famed winter sports tournaments. Whatever other qualities the music of the Northlands may have, it is always possessed of strength, vigor, and great sincerity. This reflects a people who for generations have cultivated habits of genuine honesty, healthy activity, and withal a vital self-respect.

When I Was Seventeen

Swedish grandmothers have a way of saying, "You are as full of notions as a girl of 17." This Swedish song bears out the old saying, for its traditional melody is surely whimsical and the text is as temperamental as a high school girl graduate. The poet Lilljebjorn, who wrote the words, followed the pattern of an old folk melody. "When I was 14," the girl sings, "I was always happy, but now, at 17, sometimes I am gay, sometimes sad. I do not know why, for the sky is just as blue, the grass just as green, and the cuckoo calls just as sweetly."

But this is only a girlish whim. The chorus of the song is so lighthearted, with its "tra, la la la," it is easy to guess that the singer is thinking of something very pleasant. Girls everywhere are not so different. Perhaps this is why the song is so much at home in the United States wherever girls, or their grandmothers, hear and sing it.

From Spain and Mexico

La Golondrina

The swallows of Capistrano (cap-is-trah'-no) are as much a part of California as its orange groves or Hollywood. Every spring, on St. Joseph's Day, flocks of these graceful birds come flying in from their winter home somewhere in the South Pacific. They come back to their summer nesting place under the eaves of the old Spanish Mission of Capistrano.

St. Joseph's Day is a festival day in the little town.

Children deck themselves out in their gayest clothes. From early morning every eye is on the horizon. Every ear listens for the glad cry, *"Vienen las golondrinas!"* — "The swallows are coming!" Then the bells of Capistrano ring their welcome. Everyone sings "The Swallow Song" — "La Golondrina." Birds twitter happily, as if knowing that the song and the chiming bells are especially for them.

But where does the song come from? People in California claim it for their state. Yet it is really an immigrant song. Before it was ever heard in Capistrano it found its way across the Atlantic Ocean to Mexico from sunny Spain. There, long ago, a maker of songs, Sarradel (sar-ra-del′), had asked an age-old question, "How does the bird find its way across a pathless ocean?" For his song, it is said, he used a tune he had heard among workers in the Spanish vineyards. Perhaps the workers also asked the question. The tune floats along as gracefully as a swallow's flight. It is as happy as twittering birds. Along with Sarradel, scientists have long asked that question. But the children of Capistrano feel sure that the swallows are guided from their distant winter land by the soft chimes of the mission bells carried on air waves.

When the song was first sung in Mexico, it at once became a great favorite. Now it is sung everywhere, and has even been called the "Home, Sweet Home" song of Mexico.

How did it get to California? Perhaps some gay toreador, after a successful bullfight, journeyed across the border and sang it as he rode along. Perhaps a visiting priest from Mexico taught it to the mission children. Many translations of the words differ, but the tune remains the same. From California, "La Golondrina" has traveled on wings of song to every corner of the United States.

Santa Lucia

Italy is a land of song. Everybody, from the paper boy to the Pope, makes music part of his daily life. History shows that centuries ago Pope Gregory himself wrote a book of music, which today may be seen in St. Peter's Cathedral in Rome.

Italy has some of the happiest folk songs ever written. One of these is "Santa Lucia," sung to the patron saint of Naples.

Fishermen sing "Santa Lucia" as they row out for their morning catch. The present words for the song are more like the words of a poet than of a fisherman. But the tune is a real folk song with the feel of the oars in its rhythm. Probably some long-ago poet of Italy borrowed a fisherman's tune for words of his own. But "Santa Lucia" is still a boat song known and loved far from its beautiful Bay of Naples, where it was first sung.

From the Jewish People

Both the history and the legends of the Jewish people have many beautiful stories about music. One of the best known tells how King David, when only a humble shepherd boy, played his harp and sang to Saul, the mighty king of Israel. What songs did young David sing? Another and very different legend relates that another king of the Jews, Solomon, had thousands of harpers and singers for his fabulous temple. What music did these mass groups use? Nobody knows. In those long-ago times music was not written down.

The songs for the splendid temple service were learned by rote in special schools for royal musicians. The great masses of the Jewish congregation learned the songs by hearing them repeatedly in the service.

Since the days of King Solomon, the Jews, Children of Israel, have become scattered throughout many lands. In their wanderings and their sufferings the melodies of their beautiful songs have been lost. But the words of many of them were written down and preserved forever in the *Songs of David* (The Psalms) of the Bible. A very few of the ancient traditional melodies have been remembered. These are written down and are used in all the present-day synagogues. One is "Kol Nidre." Its wistful and touching music is heard in the *Day of Atonement* ritual. For this service the holy ark is opened by two selected rabbis who take from it the Scrolls of the Hebrew Bible. From it they read aloud the "Prayer of Atonement." The cantor then sings "Kol Nidre." It is perhaps the only known music from the vast choirs of Solomon's great temple.

Although the melodies are gone, the words of the Jewish singers preserved in the Psalms have inspired the finest sacred music of the world. Bach, Handel, and a host of other musicians have set these words to music. One of the loveliest of all songs for women's voices is the trio by the Jewish composer Mendelssohn — "Lift Thine Eyes," which uses the words of the 121st Psalm. Something of the spirit and poetry of the ancient Jewish music still lives in the music of today.

ELEVEN

From Amber
to Amplification

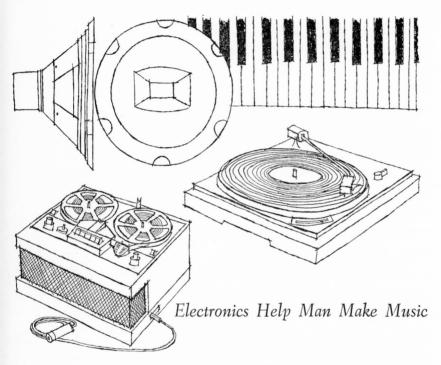

Electronics Help Man Make Music

HERE is a mystery story to rival *The Arabian Nights,* where Aladdin rubs his lamp and the genie appears to bring him magic riches. In ancient Greece, Thales (Tha-les) rubbed a piece of amber on silk and discovered not just one slave, but many. Unlike Aladdin, Thales could not see his slaves, but only what they could do. The amber caused a feather to dance, and it forced a straw to follow it across a table. Thales and his friends, "The Seven Wise Men of Greece," called these invisible magic slaves *electrons,* after *elektor,* the Greek word for amber.

WHAT CLUE DID SCIENTISTS NEED?

Those Seven Wise Men of Greece, who lived about the year 650 B. C., never did find out how the amber caused the feather and the straw to move. Although investigations continued, it was more than 2,000 years before scientists began to solve the mystery. About the year 1600, in one of the experiments, a strong force, which acted much like electrons, was given the name *electricity.* However, it was 300 years later that an Englishman finally discovered that electrons, one of the smallest particles known to science, are a vital element of electricity. Scientists needed this clue to guide them in their experiments with electricity, but it was 50 years more before they really began to find out how to use the magic powers of the tiny electrons. Through many, many years and experiments, man finally developed by 1950 the vast new science of electronics.

Today electronics serves music in many ways. It can greatly amplify the sound of musical instruments. The guitar, a humble member of the Picker family, when helped by electronics, can boom out rhythms as strong as drum beats. Through electronics, the size of musical instruments can be changed. An electric piano looks like a toy, with its largest sounding board and longest strings replaced by small electronic condensers and a pickup. Yet, even so, it can still have the volume of a concert grand. Manufacturers are constantly improving this new type of piano, but some already on the market are said to produce more accurate tones than those of the standard instruments, can be tuned more exactly, and also will stay in tune.

The pipe organ was one of the first instruments to be improved by the use of electricity. Instead of bellows, electric power runs machines that pump air, which is forced through the pipes. Also, an electric current now replaces the old, cumbersome levers that used to open and close the pipes. But, for all this electrical help, the music is still made by air vibrating in pipes, and the pipe organ is still a member of the Blower family, even though it is incorrectly called an "electric organ."

An electronic organ is an entirely different and new kind of instrument. Instead of air vibrating in pipes, the music is made by vibrating electrons created by a "tone generator." Vacuum tubes amplify these vibrations, which are electrically carried to loudspeakers to be turned into musical sounds. The organist can control these sounds electronically, so that they produce the tones of a pipe organ, or, in the same manner, he may produce the tones of a flute, a violin, or any other instrument. Instead of coming from many pipes, the sounds come from a few loudspeakers, and the volume is controlled as in a radio. An electric organ, played at full volume, can be heard a mile away. In size, this organ may be smaller than an upright piano. It may weigh less than

172

400 pounds. It is much less expensive than a pipe organ. With these advantages, the electronic organ has come to be known as "every man's organ," for it is now often found in apartments and small homes.

WHAT OTHER INSTRUMENTS HAVE BEEN CHANGED?

Another instrument, the carillon, can be entirely changed by electronics, though it would still be in the Banger family. Instead of the great, heavy bells described in Chapter II, an electronic carillon has tuned bars of steel. When struck, the tones of these are electronically amplified and carried to loud-speakers. Again, as in radio, the volume can be regulated, and the music of the carillon can still be heard far and wide.

Scrapers, too, are being changed by electronics. An electronic cello has appeared in concert. Its music, electronically amplified, filled a large hall, as the tones of an organ might do.

In all the world of music, the slaves of Thales are doing the most for the phonograph and its happy-go-lucky relative, the jukebox. These two most popular of all instruments belong to no special group. They have no family nickname. They are repeaters of music, not music makers. Yet they demonstrate a new way in which man makes music.

HOW WAS THE PHONOGRAPH DEVELOPED?

The phonograph is only about 80 years old, but its short history is packed with excitement. One summer day in 1877, in a laboratory in West Orange, New Jersey, the story began. That morning Thomas Edison gave his expert German mechanic directions for making a strange, new machine. The mechanic, who was used to making strange "contraptions," asked what this one was to be. Edison explained that this one would reproduce human speech. Shaking his head, the mechanic left the room, muttering about someone or something being "crazy."

However, by the next day he had completed the model. The new machine had a metal cylinder, with grooves that a needle would follow when the cylinder was turned by a hand-wound spring. The needle was held in a small device that contained a vibrating membrane. Attached to all this was a short tube, which ended in a hornlike bell.

The mechanic watched with amusement as Edison wrapped the cylinder in tin foil and set it turning. Then, into the bell, Edison recited, "Mary had a little lamb, its fleece was white as snow." He paused, readjusted the needle and — behold — quite distinctly from the horn came his words. *"Mein Gott in Himmel!"* gasped the mechanic, dropping into a chair. Edison himself was too amazed to speak. His machine talked! He had not even dreamed of such complete "reproduction of human speech"!

HOW DID PEOPLE REACT TO THE NEW PHONOGRAPH?

Exciting days and nights followed. Newspapers headlined, "A machine that talks!" Showmen exhibited the "miracle" at fairs and in special entertainments. In one week a single machine earned $1,800. But it was still only a *talking* machine. Then a cornetist played "Yankee Doodle" into the bell. The tune came out, with all the player's extra flourishes! The machine could make music! This was even

174

more exciting; it all but caused a riot among the listeners.

Now the business world became excited. Business companies were formed to make and sell the new machines. Scientists and engineers were hired to improve the different parts. Edison had named his invention from two Greek words, *phone* (voice) and *graphos* (to write). A rival company turned the words around and advertised "graphophones" for sale.

Edison's company was having some trouble getting musicians to make records. One German pianist, when he heard his solo played back through the machine, fainted dead away! Was he amazed or did his music sound so bad? Certainly, the early machines lacked much. They were nicknamed "screech-boxes," and were said to play "canned" music.

HOW WAS THE PHONOGRAPH IMPROVED?

Edison continued to improve his phonograph, and so did the rival companies. Soon wax replaced the tin foil on cylinders. Disks replaced the cylinders. Shellac replaced the wax. An electric motor replaced the hand-wound spring. Twenty-five years after "Mary's little lamb" came from the crude Edison horn, Caruso, the world's most famous tenor, was singing into the greatly improved machine.

WHAT DID ELDREDGE JOHNSON DO?

Then a new company appeared that was to put some kind of reproducing machine into every third home in the United States. The head of this company was Eldredge

Johnson, whose business methods almost equaled Edison's inventive genius. Johnson built huge factories, and constructed splendid recording laboratories. He paid fabulous prices to secure the finest musicians in the world to make his records. He set up an educational staff of highly trained musicians and sent them, free, on invitation, to any school or college in the United States. These people were specially trained to teach teachers how to use recorded music in the classroom, the assignment being to "help more people to hear more music."

While all this was going on, a jazz band from New Orleans made a record in Eldredge Johnson's laboratory. It made music history, and it made social history, too. Other dance bands began to make records. Someone thought of the jukebox. A New York restaurant bought one, and soon space was cleared between tables for dancing. In time, jukeboxes were added to other restaurants. Someone quipped, "The jukebox has taken the *rest* out of restaurant and put the *din* into dinner." Then records could not be produced rapidly enough. New dance steps were made up. New kinds of tunes, with new rhythms, were written.

HOW DID ELECTRONICS IMPROVE PHONOGRAPHS?

In the midst of all this, radio and, later, television were developed through the new science. But even these did not crowd out the phonograph. Slogans, such as "The tune you want when you want it," told how records continued to keep their popular place. Through electronics, better phonographs were being produced with improved amplification. Electronics helped to make much improved pickups and finer

176

records. It taught sound engineers how to record really life-like music. This gave the phonograph its modern nickname, "Hi-Fi," which means that the phonograph can reproduce with high fidelity. Best of all, the science of electronics brought the long-playing record and tape recording, which has its own fascinating story.

HOW DID BING CROSBY START A BOOM?

Crooner Bing Crosby really started a new recording history when he recorded his first radio show on tape. As the story goes, Bing did not like having to be in the studios at certain hours when, as was sometimes the case, it meant missing his dinner. Then he heard of a company that was making records with magnetic tape. He tried the new process. A broadcast from a tape recording was a great success. At once Bing formed a company, which manufactured tape-recording machines.

Bing had started a boom! Immediately, makers of electronic equipment began to produce tape recorders. Almost overnight new companies were formed. Phonograph companies added tape recorders to their products. New tapes were devised; new uses for them were discovered. Tapes of steel, paper, or plastic, coated with iron oxide, reproduce sounds with more fidelity than disks. A tape can be played back over and over. It can be erased for corrections. It can be cut and joined again, or edited to remove imperfections. Today, tape recordings furnish music for supermarkets, trains, buses, and airplanes. Tapes have been taken to the jungles of Africa, where native folk songs and the music of "talking drums" have been recorded. This music brings a vivid tone picture of jungle life; it permits modern man to picture how primitive man of long ago might have made music.

It was in a sound laboratory that the magical Electronic Music Synthesizer was developed. This synthesizer was the brain child of Dr. Harry F. Olson and his staff of RCA sound engineers. The intricate machine can produce tones like those of any musical instrument, or of the human voice. It can be made to produce combinations of voices and instruments never before sounded together. Dr. Olson and his staff believe that, as they perfect the synthesizer, they will also change the whole art of music making.

IN WHAT OTHER WAYS CAN ELECTRONICS AID MUSIC?

The science of electronics can aid music in other ways. Back in the age of the Cremona violin makers, Stradivarius selected the wood for his instruments. Modern violin makers now use an electronic hearing device, by which they can measure the density of the wood they use. So, through electronics, what has been impossible — to produce a violin as beautiful in tone and design as a Stradivarius — may become possible. Some painstaking violin maker of Chicago or San Francisco may produce another $65,000 violin.

From the amber of Thales to the amplification of music today is a long and wonderful story. An even more magic tale may yet remain for the future. Sounds now too high or too low for mortal ears may be electronically captured, carried, amplified, and brought within the range of man's hearing. Some fine morning, the sound of an opening rosebud may add the beauty of a new music to the garden!

178

To a person listening to a musical performance on an ordinary radio or phonograph, all the voices and instruments come from the same source. The reason is that the sounds produced by any group of performers are gathered by microphones and transmitted to the listener over a single sound track and reproduced in his home through a single loudspeaker.

In a concert hall the waves of sound move along straight lines from the different voices and instruments to the ears of the listener and are therefore heard as coming from several different directions. That is one reason why music heard in a live performance usually sounds better than the same performance reproduced over a radio or phonograph.

With the new type of sound reproduction known as stereophonic recording, it is possible to bring to the listener in his home much of the realism of an actual performance. This is accomplished by the use at every stage of the process of two or more separate sound channels. Separate microphones capture the sounds coming from different directions, electronic devices record the different sounds in separate tracks on tapes or discs, and the stereophonic phonograph reproduces the original sounds through separate speakers.

When the speakers are properly spaced and the listener properly situated with relation to them, he hears the reproduced sounds from two or more sources corresponding to the different directions from which the sounds of the original performance would reach a listener in a concert hall. The result closely duplicates the realism of a live performance.

TWELVE

From Tribal Song to Symphony

Highlights of United States Music

WHAT songs, what pictures, what stories make up a musical panorama of the United States! From age-old Indian tom-tom and tribal songs to the radio and television concerts of today, the story spans several centuries.

In a primitive Indian village hundreds of years ago, squaws roasted venison over open fires, while braves fashioned arrowheads of flint. A visitor from a distant tribe arrived on this scene. After welcoming him and giving him food, the Indians seated themselves around him and asked, "Have you brought us any songs?"

The guest sang to the villagers of the wind. The words of his song were chanted to a few tones, which followed each other strangely.

Bejin (One) No din (Wind)
Ningo (I am) Nawendan (Master of it)

The guest sang his song again and again, and the braves finally joined him. A throbbing tom-tom in the background gave a feeling of strength and mastery to the song.

The "Wind Song" passed from Indian father to Indian son. Generations later it was recorded for the Bureau of Ethnology. And some day perhaps a United States composer may borrow its chanting tune to lend strength to his own kind of music.

WHAT INDIAN CEREMONIAL SONGS HAVE BEEN RECORDED?

The story of some other Indian songs began with daybreak in a pueblo village on a high mesa in the Southwest. The Sun Priest stood on the flat roof of the highest adobe house. Behind him, an attendant struck chimes on a large metal plate. As the first sunbeams reached the mesa, the Priest sang, "Rise, arise, arise!" While daylight flooded the mesa, the Sun Priest offered up his morning prayer-song to the Sun God. It was repeated from every housetop.

This was the day for the ancient Rain Ceremony. The tribe assembled, and from pueblo and mesa the smoke of the ceremonial fire rose through golden air to the blue sky. White-clad, copper-skinned Indian girls sang as they danced to the invocation. Hour after hour they continued, to the steady throb of the tom-tom. Stars replaced the sun. Suddenly there was a joyous cry, "Clouds arise! Hail them!" While welcome rain drenched the land, the Ceremonial Song of Thanksgiving rose jubilantly.

WHO WROTE DOWN THESE INDIAN SONGS?

Many years later these Indian songs of the Southwest were written down by Carlos Troyer, who gave them piano accompaniments that imitate chime plate and tom-tom. Now children in all parts of the United States can find these ancient ceremonial songs in school songbooks.

WHAT SONGS DID EARLY SETTLERS BRING HERE?

Legend, poem, and history all attest to the fact that Plymouth Colony was founded with a song.

> *Amidst the storm they sang,*
> *And the stars heard and the sea!*
> *And the sounding aisles of the dim woods rang*
> *To the anthem of the free!*

So wrote Felicia Hemans in her poem, "The Landing of the Pilgrim Fathers." Another account tells how, even in great peril, the Pilgrims "refreshed themselves by singing."

The early settlers along our Atlantic shores sang English

182

songs. It was almost a century and a half before Americans found time for making their own music. Those were years of hunting for food, of fighting Indians, of clearing land, of building homes and towns and roads, of seeding and harvesting. Still, there was singing. Every shipload of newcomers brought their native songs — Dutch, French, Scandinavian, Italian, and Spanish.

WHAT IS THE STORY OF "YANKEE DOODLE"?

Probably some time before the Revolutionary War, the first little American tune was written. It was made up of strains from different Old World lands, united in one New World melody. There is a bit from an English nursery tune, part of a Dutch harvest song, a snatch from some Italian or Spanish folk dance, blended in one melody, a quick step that fairly shouts, "Forward, march!" "Yankee Doodle" it was called. Nobody knows why. But, in spite of its silly words, United States armies have fifed this spirited tune through stiff battles to victory. There was that day in 1775 after the "Midnight Ride of Paul Revere" when "Yankee Doodle" played the prelude to the Revolutionary War, and it continued to give spirit to the colonial armies during the six years of war.

WHAT OTHER SONGS WERE WRITTEN?

In the difficult years after the war, most of the music Americans played and sang was still that of the Old World. Francis Scott Key, in 1814, did write a fiery patriotic song that gave the United States flag a poetic name, "The Star-

Spangled Banner." It was, and is, sung to the tune of an English drinking song. In 1832 Samuel Smith wrote the words of "My Country 'Tis of Thee," which gave the United States a special name, "Land of Liberty." Although the words and spirit were American, the music was not; it was borrowed from a German folk tune.

WHAT SONGS WERE NEGROES MAKING?

All this time, on the plantations of the South, Negro slaves were making songs of their own. What did these slaves from Africa sing about? There were no "broadspears" to praise, in their favorite answer-song manner, with the tribal leader singing the story and at the end of each line waiting for a chorus of praise from his listeners.

These slaves had no stories. They had even forgotten their own language. They could neither read nor write. But a new source for songs did develop. Some few "house servants" heard Bible stories. In rare instances, some learned to read the Bible. The other slaves, hungry for stories, listened eagerly as the Bible stories were repeated to them.

HOW WERE SPIRITUALS WRITTEN?

Sometimes a storyteller became a preacher. In his own dramatic manner and language, he told the Bible story about Elijah being carried to heaven in a chariot of fire. "Gold like fiahr, up in de clouds! Hosses like fiahr! De chariot of Israel an' de hosses der of!" When he paused, "Singin' Joseph" sprang to his feet. His voice, vibrant as the deep tones of a cello, rang out, "Swing low, sweet chariot!" Like a trained choir, the listeners responded, "Comin' fo' to ca'y me home."

184

Again the voice of Joseph, "Swing low, sweet chariot," and again the choir, "Comin' fo' to ca'y me home." Now, Joseph had a new thought, "I looked ovah Jordan, an' what did I see." Like a mighty pipe organ came the response, "Comin' fo' to ca'y me home." With mounting triumph, Joseph sang, "A band of angels comin' aftah me."

WHAT MIGHT BE THE STORY OF "BY-AN'-BY"?

Another famous Negro song could have been written in this way. A young worker in a cotton field stopped to listen to a redbird's song and echoes of a mockingbird. The Negro matched the sounds with a song of his own. "Oh-by-an'-by," he sang, "I take-a ma wings an' I cleave-a de air." He liked his song and repeated it over and over, "Oh-by-an'-by. . . ." Beside him, a bent old Negro caught up the strain. But his sack hung heavy, and its drag crept into his answering refrain, "Oh-by-an'-by, by-an'-by I's a-gonna lay down ma heavy load." Now the young slave sang, "On a mornin' bright an' fair I feels lak a eagle in de air." But always at the end of his line, as his tribal ancestors had done, he waited for the bent old Negro's "by-an'-by, by-an'-by I's gonna lay down mah heavy load." Other workers joined in the refrain. Today people in all parts of the world listen, often spellbound, to the now famous "By-an'-By" folk song, which long ago evolved from the souls of Negro slaves.

Such songs lifted the hearts of humble Negroes. They came to be known as spirituals because they told of the inner hopes of the slaves. They expressed hopes for a better future in the world to come, and are among the finest folk-art songs ever produced.

In another part of the South a very different music was being sung. Sometimes, in the beginning of United States history, venturesome people left the coast settlements to make their homes in the wild Appalachian ranges. Their Old World songs went with them. Years passed, and these pioneers found themselves established in a rugged "penned-in-land." Beyond their isolated cabins, America changed, but they still held to hand hoe, spinning wheel, and tallow candle. They were without books or schools. Yet there was singing. Nights when the air was sweet with honeysuckle and mountain laurel, there were "gatherin's" about cabin doors. The mountain folk sang old ballads their forefathers had sung long ago in Wales or Scotland, and English songs from Shakespeare's time. They made new story-songs of happenings in their own mountains, too, songs such as "Coaxin' Polly" and "Sourwood Mountain."

These were quaint, humble music makers, yet they inspired one of the foremost composers of the United States, Aaron Copland. His ballet suite, *Appalachian Spring*, won him the Pulitzer Prize and the Music Critics' Award for 1944. The mountain songs are often imitated on the stage and in best-selling records, and many times not too creditably. The real appeal of this music is its simple beauty and its close association with the lives of people who made it.

WHAT SONGS DID PRAIRIE PIONEERS MAKE?

Beyond the Appalachians, in the frontier farming communities of Illinois, Wisconsin, and Iowa, different songs were being made. At corn-husking time, men and women circled through the figures of the square dance and sang the all-American tunes of "Turkey in the Straw," "Old Dan Tucker," and "Arkansas Traveler."

WHAT SONGS DID STEPHEN FOSTER WRITE?

While the mountain singers made their own special "hurting" songs and the pioneers made gay dancing tunes, Stephen Collins Foster was making still different songs for the United States. Foster made songs for the great and the humble, for the wise and for the foolish, and for the gay and the sad. Because these songs can be sung by everybody, they are often called folk songs. But, in whatever classification, no American songs have yet approached the popularity of "Old Folks at Home" and "My Old Kentucky Home." Then, too, there are "Jeanie with the Light Brown Hair," "Old Black Joe," and "Oh! Susannah." Since Foster made the "Swanee" River famous, "The Old Folks" has traveled "all up an' down de whole creation," and, more than any of his other 200 songs, helped to give Foster the title he long held, "Favorite song writer of the United States."

WHAT SONGS DID THE COWBOYS MAKE?

Quite another kind of folk music grew up on the Western plains. In the old days every cowboy outfit had its songs, which the cowboys made to their own liking. Sometimes they borrowed a tune and adapted it to new words. One favorite song was "Home on the Range." Others were "The Chisholm Trail," "Poor Lonesome Cowboy," and "The Lone Star Trail."

187

Some of the best tunes, as well as the words, were made up by the boys as they rode in the lonely nights when never a fence nor a road crossed the wide "prairie-e." The lonely cowboy sang to his long-horned cattle because it helped to pass away the time and tended to quiet the herd. He had no songbook, so he made up words and a tune of his own to go with them. "Git Along, Little Dogies," sometimes called a cattle lullaby, is a good example of a song made up in this way. The tune goes along like the slow jog of a cow pony. Nobody knows who first sang it, but it is easy to imagine that it might have been in some such way as this.

A great herd moved toward the river. Long slanting rays of the afternoon sun shone through the dust that rose from thousands of hoofs and made a haze above the moving cattle.

The day was hot, and the cattle were thirsty. Leaders of the herd smelled the water of the river. But the dogies (do'-gies), the little motherless calves, smelled only dust and lagged behind. The cowpuncher talked to the laggards.

"Git along there, it's not my fault you're orphans, git along there, you dogies!" Then he gave his cattle call, a long drawn-out, half-sung, "Whoopie Ti Yi Yo." Then he made a tune to go with his call and sang, "Whoopie Ti Yi Yo, git along little dogie, it's your misfortune an' none of my own."

The fall of the pony's feet on the turf beat out a steady jog, jog rhythm. The cowboy made up more lines:

> Whoopie Ti yi yo, git along little dogies,
> You know that Wyoming will be your new home.

Later, other cowboys in other outfits would hear the song. More verses would be added. Some 20 now tell the story of the dogies and their boys from Texas all the way up to Wyoming pasture lands.

HOW DID MUSIC INTERESTS GROW AROUND 1900?

Toward the close of the 19th century, people in the United States had more leisure time — time that could be devoted to making and enjoying music. In the larger cities special concert halls were built, where large audiences could hear visiting musicians present the great music of the world. In many smaller communities, Chautauqua groups presented programs during the summer months.

Throughout the land people were singing the melodious songs from the light operas of Reginald de Koven and Victor Herbert. Art songs such as Nevin's "The Rosary," Speaks' "Sylvia," Cadman's "At Dawning," and many more were favorites.

In towns, and even in cities, minstrel shows were as popular as today's movies or television shows. Men singers "blacked up" to look like Negroes, played the banjo, shook the "bones," sang comic songs, and told funny jokes. "Dixie," a favorite minstrel song, has earned its right to its own story, which follows this chapter.

Two of our country's great patriotic songs came from this period: Julia Ward Howe's "The Battle Hymn of the Republic" and Katherine Lee Bates' "America the Beautiful." The stirring music of the "Battle Hymn" is equally well suited to Miss Howe's words, "Mine eyes have seen the glory of the coming of the Lord; He is trampling out the vintage where the grapes of wrath are stor'd," or to the tragedy of

189

"John Brown's body lies a-mould'ring in the grave, His soul goes marching on!"

WHAT TRIUMPH DID EDWARD MACDOWELL HAVE?

The year 1896 was a triumphant one for a young American composer, Edward MacDowell. In that year he became head of the music department at Columbia University; also the Boston Symphony, then the leading symphony orchestra in the United States, presented two of his major compositions on the same program. One of these selections, *The Indian Suite,* uses Indian melodies and rhythm, which drew the attention of other composers to the primitive strength and beauty of Indian music.

WHAT SONGS DID MACDOWELL WRITE?

Each summer MacDowell and his wife sought refuge in the quiet of the New Hampshire hills. In a small cabin studio, tucked away amidst thick trees and hazel growth, MacDowell gave his keyboard messages to the world. His music was the type that many could play and all could enjoy: "From an Indian Lodge," "To a Wild Rose," and "To a Water Lily." MacDowell put Uncle Remus and Bre'r Rabbit to music, and transcribed the dancing "Will o' the Wisp" and the chattering "By Meadow Brook" for the piano. In his "Witches' Dance," MacDowell displayed his understanding of the wee folk and fairies. He heard music in moonlight and shadow; he found melody in field and flower; and he knew how to transcribe what he heard for the piano that others might share this magic. To do such simple things so exquisitely required true genius, and MacDowell, in his compositions, willed to the world a true heritage of America's music.

At the turn of the century, many American composers went to Europe for training, but they returned to America, where they wrote in original styles. Not only were these men composers, but many were also teachers, conductors, critics, and authors.

WHO WAS HORATIO PARKER?

One of these was Horatio Parker, who served as head of the Department of Music at Yale University, and also led a busy life as teacher, conductor, and composer. His talents were many and varied, and he wrote equally well for instruments, keyboard, and voice. Parker is frequently credited with creating a demand for American music.

WHO WERE OTHER AMERICAN COMPOSERS OF THE TIME?

A great many other Americans were writing music. Charles Ives and John Alden Carpenter were outstanding because they were willing to experiment with music and refused to be dominated by one style of composition. Harry T. Burleigh and Nathaniel Dett composed music based on Negro folk songs, while Harvey Loomis and Charles Wakefield Cadman turned to Indian music for their inspiration.

In the United States, there was more musical freedom than in Europe. Our people were eager for and receptive toward new ideas, and the compositions of American composers were so varied that one can only say our music was written by Americans for Americans.

WHAT MUSIC WAS POPULAR DURING AND AFTER
WORLD WAR I?

During World War I President Woodrow Wilson, firm in his belief in the power of music as a morale booster, ordered a great many young men to be trained to direct and play in army bands. And John Philip Sousa, the March King, led his United States Marine Band down Fifth Avenue in New York in a Liberty Loan parade; men bared their heads as the flag passed to the accompaniment of Sousa's famous march, "The Stars and Stripes Forever." George M. Cohan led America in other music, famous war songs such as "Over There" and "Tipperary."

After the war, some famous musical shows were written by Americans: *Show Boat*, by Jerome Kern, and *Maytime*, by Sigmund Romberg.

WHAT DID DAMROSCH DO?

Still another man came to the forefront of American music. He was Walter Damrosch, who exerted untold influence upon the youth of America through his radio programs. These programs were heard in thousands of classrooms across the country and, by radio, Damrosch was able to present the music of the masters in an interesting, authentic manner.

192

George Gershwin was yet another American musical genius. Although a product of Tin Pan Alley, Gershwin possessed the peculiar ability to blend elements of jazz and classical music in his compositions with great effectiveness. From 1919 to 1933, Gershwin wrote musical comedies for Broadway. After this era, he turned to more serious work. In 1924, at the request of Paul Whiteman, he wrote his famous "Rhapsody in Blue." And Whiteman, in turn, performed the work in Carnegie Hall. The most important work of Gershwin was what is considered to be a true American opera, *Porgy and Bess,* which was produced in 1935.

WHAT WERE SOME OTHER MILESTONES?

The year 1927 opened up whole new vistas to American composers. It was then that the first successful talking picture appeared — *The Jazz Singer,* with Al Jolson.

During World War II an American popular composer, Irving Berlin, turned out a "hit" tune. This was "White Christmas." Although Berlin has written more than a thousand songs, none has equaled the success of this tune, which is supposed to have sold 3 million copies. In 1957 Berlin completed his fiftieth year of successful song writing.

WHAT PLACES IN THE EAST CAN ONE VISIT ON A MUSICAL TOUR OF THE U. S.?

In a musical tour of the United States, one might visit many places and hear many famous composers, conductors, and musicians. In the beautiful Berkshire Hills, at the Festival of Tanglewood, one might hear Howard Hanson, one of America's eminent composers and educators, conduct members of the Boston Symphony Orchestra in a performance of his *Nordic Symphony*. Hanson has been head of the Eastman School of Music since 1924 and has built Eastman into one of the finest music schools in the world. No longer is it necessary for Americans to go to Europe for excellent musical training; in fact, the contrary is true: Europeans are now coming here to study.

In New York City, you could see the latest Broadway musical, attend performances by the Metropolitan Opera, the New York City Opera, or the American Opera Society; hear excellent solo recitals, as well as concerts by the Philharmonic Orchestra and the Symphony of the Air.

WHAT ARE FAMOUS MUSIC CENTERS OF THE MIDWEST?

In a modern camp, in a wooded glade, between two lakes, hundreds of boys and girls are making music, studying drama, dancing, working with radio. This is the famous Interlochen Music Camp in Michigan, founded in 1926 by the beloved music educator, Dr. Joseph Maddy. Interlochen is the culmination of Dr. Maddy's dream of a place where boys and girls from every state could come together in the summer to study and play and learn about great music.

In Chicago, one might see Fritz Reiner conduct one of the world's finest symphony orchestras, or see a production by the Lyric Opera. In the summer you may hear the Chicago Symphony play at the Ravinia Festival. In St. Louis one

194

might attend the Municipal Opera and at Indiana University at Bloomington, you might attend the annual Palm Sunday performance of Wagner's *Parsifal*.

WHERE TO GO IN THE WEST?

In Central City, Colorado, a ballet company might be performing Aaron Copland's *Appalachian Spring*. In the Hollywood Bowl, it could be Morton Gould conducting his own orchestra in his composition, the *Americana Suite*. At the Santa Fe Opera in New Mexico, you might be fortunate in seeing Igor Stravinsky conducting his operas and choral works. And if you are in Dallas or San Francisco during their opera season, you will enjoy an evening there, listening to world-famous operatic stars.

AND WHAT ABOUT THE EVERYDAY MUSIC OF AMERICANS?

Almost every town or city of any size has a municipal band, and frequently a civic orchestra. Throughout the country there are hundreds of bands and choruses in the schools. Farm Bureau choruses, as well as glee clubs of every kind can be found throughout the United States.

How a Modern Man Made
a Song

The Story of "Dixie"

YOUNG Dan Emmett earned his living by being funny. He was "end-man" in a minstrel show, which, long before a comedy film made people laugh, was the funniest show anywhere to be seen. The end-man was the funniest part of the show. He must tell a story in a way that would set sober sides shaking. He must dance a clog that would start even a deacon's feet a-tapping, and his banjo and bones must turn any dirge into a cakewalk.

Dan Emmett could do all this and more. The foolish songs he made up for the minstrel show "walk-'round" would set the audience into such roars of laughter that the men of the troupe dubbed them the "hooray songs."

But one season Dan Emmett just couldn't be funny. He had come up from a trip through the sunny South, and the cold of the North was getting on his nerves. He was doing his best to amuse his New York audience and, what was more important, his manager. But sometimes he was even afraid he would lose his job. He just couldn't get a smile out of life, which was most unusual for Dan Emmett.

On one stormy Saturday night when he was feeling particularly low, the manager came to him and said, "Emmett, we'll have to have a new hooray song right away. You get one ready for rehearsal Monday morning."

Monday morning! It was then late Saturday night. But the manager was not to be put off. "Monday morning for rehearsal," he insisted.

196

Downhearted, Dan Emmett turned toward his lodging-house. The wind of the street set him shivering. With a disgusted shrug he exclaimed, "New York! Oh, I wish I was in Dixie!" As he hurried along he repeated the wish over and over to himself until without knowing it he was half singing the words in time to his hurrying footsteps.

The next morning at his window, looking down upon the cold, wet street with its hurrying crowds, he again remembered the balmy days of the Southland and he again repeated, "I wish I was in Dixie." This time he said it aloud and as he said it he beat an impatient tattoo upon the rain-flecked windowpane. Unconsciously he repeated the words and the tattoo, and unconsciously he fitted them to the rhythm of his quick steps of the night before — "I wish I was in Dixie!"

Days of sunshine — nights of song — in Dixie. The words were a sort of magic. The end-man forgot the cold New York street. He forgot that he had to make a new song. He was hearing the punk-a-punk of the banjo strings. He was hearing the singing Negroes. He was roaming over a sunny plantation lawn. Hooray, to live and die in Dixie!

Suddenly the end-man stopped. His lips puckered into a whistle. The hooray song! He had it! "To live and die in Dixie!" That would make a hooray song worth singing!

The rhythm of his quick steps as he had hurried along the night before belonged with the idea, so the tune, of course, had the stirring beat of a quick step mingled with the punk-a-punk of banjos. The melody that came to Dan Emmett had the smile of the South and the swing of a New York street crowd. And so, on a bleak day in a northern city, "Dixie," the famous song of the sunny South, was born.

Monday morning at rehearsal the men of the troupe pronounced the new song a "rouser," and the manager said, "I knew you could do it."

Monday night Dan Emmett with banjo and bones sang "Dixie" for the walk-'round, and the people cheered, just as people have ever since, whenever and wherever "Dixie" is heard.

The words are nonsense, but the jolly tune has kept the song a favorite when most of the other walk-'rounds of the old days have been forgotten. The swinging melody and the dancing rhythm set every heart beating happily, and everyone agrees with the Negro orator who once said, " 'Dixie' is a chune that can git up an' walk eroun' by itself!"

That was the very kind of tune the southern bandmaster needed when the North and the South went into the war of the sixties. But instead of being sung with banjo and bones, the tune was played by fife and drum. It made a wonderful soldier-march, and soon every man, woman, and child of the South was singing "Dixie." It became the war cry of the southern armies.

The people of the North loved "Dixie," too. When at last the war was over, President Lincoln knew that the jolly little tune would be a real peacemaker. He had it played often in Washington, and North and South listened with mingled smiles and tears. So "Dixie" healed deep wounds and eased old scars, and became the darling of a united nation.

But for all the fame of his song, Dan Emmett received very little money for it. He had let it go for only a small amount, so while it was selling by thousands its popularity brought him not a penny. In his old age when he could no longer work, he had to live as best he could on gifts of food and clothing. Yet in those hard years Dan Emmett still kept his love for fun and for song. Often when a show troupe came to his home town, Mt. Vernon, Ohio, he would manage to make friends with the doorkeeper and have a free seat to hear the new songs. His happiest moment was when, as sometimes happened, "Dixie" was sung or played by the company band. It was then that the old end-man forgot his troubles and lived again the triumphs of his better days.

One evening as he hobbled down the village street, he discovered that a company he had once known was to show that night at the opera house. It was a musical comedy and the old end-man forgot his stiff joints in his eagerness to hear the jolly songs. He had no money, but he was sure the manager would remember him, and he tottered up to the ticket window to ask for admission. But the manager was not there. A brisk young stranger shook his head, "Sorry, sir, no free seats tonight."

But something in the eyes of the old man as he turned away caught the attention of the ticket seller. He asked a lad standing near who the old man might be. "That's Dan Emmett," the boy told him. "He used to be a comedian, a band man, and a song writer, but his songs never made him any money and now he's down and out."

The manager was passing and caught the name. "Dan Emmett!" he exclaimed. "Go bring the old gentleman back. He shall be our guest tonight."

From the front row the stooped old man watched and listened attentively. At each number his eyes brightened. Yet at the close a shade passed over his face. "Dixie" had not even been used as an encore.

But the curtain was up again. The whole company had assembled on the stage. They came to the very front and turned toward Don Emmett. The band struck into "Dixie!"

The manager signed for Dan Emmett to rise. How the people clapped! The stooping spine straightened. His little hooray song, as fresh and jolly as on its first night! The trembling limbs grew steady.

The Dan Emmett who stood there was strangely different from the old man who two hours before had turned away from the ticket window. The faded eyes were shining. The trembling lips smiled happily. What if people did give him food and clothing? He had given them a song — a song that would never grow old; a song that had helped to bring peace after war; a song that was the darling of his country. The bowed head lifted proudly. He was no longer Dan Emmett a poor old man, he was Dan Emmett the author and composer of "Dixie!"

THIRTEEN

Jazz

Americans Create a New Music Style

THIS is the story of a totally different kind of music — music so distinctive that it could only have come from a people not bound by conventional styles. It is the story of jazz, the one style of music that is completely original in the United States.

The time is midmorning of an early summer day during the "gay nineties." The scene is the city of New Orleans. Stopping to listen, one hears only ordinary sounds — the clop-clop of horses pulling wagons and carriages, the closing of doors, the humming of bees, the warbling of birds.

But, suddenly, music fills the air — the high, clear notes of a cornet, the rippling of a clarinet, the driving tones of a trombone, the grunt of a bass, and the boom of a drum. A horse-drawn wagon rounds a corner. Seated in it are several Negroes, dressed in high-collared red coats, blue hats, and white trousers. A sign on the wagon reads, "Buddy Bolden's Ragtime Band, playing tonight at Johnson Park."

Everyone stops to listen to the throbbing rhythm. A Negro newsboy puts down his papers and, with nimble feet, beats out a brisk buck-and-wing. Other people tap their feet, nod their heads, or clap their hands.

This joyous music comes straight from the hearts of the players, for the men have never taken music lessons and cannot read a note. They play as they feel — with spontaneity and freedom.

WHO CREATED THE JAZZ STYLE?

Jazz seems to have had its origin in New Orleans at the close of the 19th century. To understand why it originated when and where it did, we must know something of the history of the people who gave it birth — the American Negroes.

202

When the Negroes came to the New World as slaves, they brought their work songs and ceremonial songs with them. These songs were blended into one of the most popular forms of jazz — the blues. Just as work songs were stories of commonplace events, the blues were likewise about ordinary activities and emotions — sleeping, eating, fear, love.

HOW DID BRASS BANDS CONTRIBUTE TO JAZZ?

It was in the colorful brass bands that jazz was born. These bands developed the principal elements of jazz— freedom to improvise, and syncopation, or a temporary shifting of the rhythmic accent from strong to weak beats.

As early as 1853 these Negro brass and marching bands were found in the South. Not only did they perform at picnics, meetings, and clambakes, but they served a peculiar function to the traditions of New Orleans and played for funerals. A band would meet at the home of the deceased and lead the funeral procession to the cemetery, playing familiar hymns and "dead marches."

The return trip was different. A block from the cemetery gates the drummer would break into a faster rhythm. The band would strike up "When the Saints Go Marching In" or "Oh, Didn't He Ramble," and the erstwhile mourners would dance back to the center of town in joyous confusion.

The "Onward and Upward Brass Band," the "Diamond Stone," and the "Excelsior" were but a few of the famous old brass bands in which many of the "great" men in jazz started their careers.

Congo Square, a flat, dusty field on Rampart Street in New Orleans, made its own contribution to the development of jazz. It was there that the Negroes gathered on Saturday and Sunday nights to dance. Several Negroes beat on an old pork barrel or dry-goods box, while a few onlookers sang and chanted. To this primitive music, the Negroes danced for hours — writhing, swaying, twisting, and leaping until exhausted. Newly arrived slaves from Africa participated, bringing about a further blending of work songs, spirituals, blues, and ceremonial songs into the exciting form of jazz.

At the end of the Civil War, northern troops abandoned in the South some equipment, including musical instruments, which fell into the eager hands of a few musical Negroes. These Negroes, now free to do as they pleased, learned to play these instruments, not in the sense of reading notes, but with the idea of expressing the wild, innate musical feelings with which they were so richly blessed. It was easy for them to learn to "blow the blues."

WHAT IS A "BLUES" SONG?

The simple harmonies and slower tempos of the blues offered early jazz players a little more time to think about their improvisations. The blues song is a twelve-measure tune in four-four time, with a simple chord structure that can be varied and played in major or minor keys. Around the blues harmonies, jazz musicians have improvised thousands of tunes.

Another jazz style of the somewhat later period was "ragtime." The Negro borrowed freely from the dance tunes of the day. The mazurka, the quadrille, the cakewalk, all became the basis of ragtime music. This style made use of faster tempos than the blues and was basically a steady "two-beats to the bar" rhythm in the bass, while the melody was highly syncopated. In New Orleans the piano player also "ragged" the bass, playing syncopated figures in the bass with the left hand against a different syncopated beat with the right hand. Once a player had this feeling for syncopation against syncopation, he had at his command the basic material for a real jazz style.

The "great" period of jazz started in New Orleans about 1890. The public had grown tired of dancing the old style of dances, most of which had been borrowed from Europe. They wanted a new and more expressive type of music that would offer them more freedom and activity. Jazz gave them what they wanted.

As musicians improvised the music, the dancers made up new dances. From the "gay nineties" through the "roaring twenties" jazz grew and exerted a tremendous influence in the United States.

HOW DID JAZZ CONTRIBUTE TO LANGUAGE?

From this new music style, there developed a richly descriptive vocabulary. Musicians "borrowed" words, and a "new language" emerged, making strange sounds, such as "He's a solid cat and sure sends 'em with his breaks." To

205

the initiated, this meant "This fellow is a good jazz musician and he has a certain appeal to an audience when playing by himself in solo passages." Those "in the know" were called "cats." Less fortunate individuals might be referred to as "squares."

WHAT ARE THE MAIN FEATURES OF JAZZ TODAY?

The basic features of jazz, as we know it today, are a "solid beat," a rhythm of four beats to the bar or measure. This rhythm is set up by the rhythm section, which may consists of drums, piano, bass, and guitar. Above this is the "off-beat," or the other instruments, such as saxophones, clarinets, trumpets, and trombones, playing syncopated figures.

To add still more "drive" and "push," or "punch," some members may set up "riffs" under a soloist. These riffs are consistent rhythm figures that add tension to the music merely by being repeated.

WHAT IS THE BIG FACTOR IN GOOD JAZZ?

The big factor in good jazz is the ability of the person playing the melody to improvise on it, while others improvise parts that fit the melody. When a player takes a "break," he plays a short solo, without the support of the other players. These "breaks" afford the jazz player a chance to show ingenuity and creativeness on his instrument.

WHO WAS THE LEADER IN THE EARLY JAZZ BANDS?

In early jazz bands, the cornetist or trumpet player was the leader, and it was usually he who introduced and carried

206

the melody. Around this melody the clarinetist and trombonist improvised their parts in harmony, while the rhythm instruments — tuba, banjo (or guitar), and drums — beat out the time. Frequently, each performer took a turn at the melody while the other players supplied the background. This led to all sorts of variations in the melody, and provided much of the spark that made jazz different from music performed from a written score.

WHAT EFFECT DID "JAM SESSIONS" HAVE ON JAZZ?

The story of jazz would not be complete without men tioning "jam sessions." Jazz musicians, a clannish lot, often got together after their regular "jobs" to play just for "kicks." In these jam sessions, the musicians would play for hours, going from one tune to another, improvising their parts and getting musical ideas from each other.

It was there, in smoke-filled rooms, with a few fortunate friends swaying in rhythm, that new harmonies were tried out, notes were flatted and added, and the "blue" note, a note not in the basic chord structure, was emphasized. Muted effects, glissandos, smears, and blends became a part of jazz. At these sessions, the already exciting jazz vocabulary was further enriched.

HOW DID JAZZ STYLES DIFFER?

If the music was high, fast and loud, played with a "jump" beat, it was called "hot." "Sweet" music, in direct contrast, was generally played in medium or slow tempos, in a soft, relaxed style. "Dirty" music referred to rough treatment of a song, with somewhat discordant harmonies and special effects, such as "growling" trumpets, "squealing" clarinets, and "blasting" trombones.

HOW DID JAZZ TRAVEL TO OTHER PLACES?

In 1910 Captain Joseph Streckfus, owner of many of the big Mississippi paddle-wheelers, decided that he wanted musicians on his boats who could play jazz. Many of the fine jazz musicians were lured to the big river boats with the promise of steady salaries. In this way jazz traveled up the Mississippi and its major tributaries to St. Louis, Memphis, Kansas City, Louisville, and Davenport.

When the big river boats tied up in these cities, the musicians went ashore to sit in jam sessions with local musicians. In this manner, it was only a few short years before jazz, from its simple beginnings in New Orleans, had spread to the heartland of America, and from there throughout the country.

WHEN WAS JAZZ INTRODUCED TO CHICAGO?

In 1915 "Tom Brown's Dixieland Jazz Band" introduced jazz to Chicago. Two years later Joseph "King" Oliver traveled to Chicago with his band. Almost overnight, he became a "smash hit." For years he was regarded as the King of Jazz.

The big, brawny city of Chicago opened its arms to jazz. Lured by the ready acceptance of jazz by Chicagoans and the high rate of pay, many of the best players from New Orleans went there.

In 1922 "King" Oliver sent to New Orleans for a young

trumpet player named Louis Armstrong. Louie soon surpassed the "King," and is now known as the world's greatest jazz trumpeter. He is also one of America's finest good-will ambassadors, because of his personality and his ability to interpret his type of music for people of many nationalities.

During the twenties jazz made itself popular in many parts of the world. However, not all listeners were convinced that jazz was a good thing. At the same time that jazz was making friends, it was also creating strong enemies, who claimed that this music was a bad influence on the youth of the world.

WHEN DID JAZZ BEGIN TO FADE OUT?

With the depression of 1929 and the dismal years following, the popularity of jazz began to wane. Ballrooms and dance halls closed, and many musicians drifted into other jobs.

WHAT TREND LATER TOOK PLACE?

When America recovered enough to resume some of its pleasures, the trend in music was toward the big band. Composed of from 10 to 18 musicians, the big band played special arrangements written for it. These bands became known for their distinctive styles.

Jimmy Lunceford, Count Basie, Duke Ellington, and Benny Goodman had "swing" bands. These bands were well rehearsed and played with attention to detail. Solos were written or memorized so that each time the band played a selection, the solo would sound the same. Little opportunity was afforded any individual to improvise unless he was the leader of a band built around his own special talents. The big bands were exploited — they were showpieces. Swing was the thing, but people came more to listen than to dance. And eventually they grew tired of listening.

WHEN DID JAZZ REGAIN ITS POPULARITY?

Once again New Orleans jazz came into its own. In the mid-forties, old-time jazz men Bunk Johnson, Kid Ory, Mutt Carey, George Lewis, and many others came out of retirement. A wave of enthusiasm swept over the general public, and people recognized the mastery of the musicians who could interpret this New Orleans "Dixieland" style.

For a short period in the forties, bop, or bebop, was regarded as a new form of jazz. This style was much more dissonant than early jazz, and the melody was harder to follow. Bop depended on improvisation, but because it was harder to listen to and understand, it never attained lasting popularity.

Another form of jazz was the sound that Stan Kenton named "progressive." This was the big band sound, meticulously rehearsed, with emphasis on new combinations of notes and dissonance.

WHAT TYPE OF MUSIC DO COMBOS PLAY?

Lately, the trend has been once again toward smaller bands, or combos, of three to six men. The style of these new combos is referred to as "cool" jazz, a form that emphasizes a relaxed sound rather than the driving and blasting of so-called "hot" music. Rhythms are intricate and involved, and in many cases show the effects of the serious musical training that many of the "cool" jazz players have had.

WHAT ONE THING CHARACTERIZES JAZZ?

The one thing that has always been characteristic of jazz is that its musicians seek new sounds, new rhythms, and new combinations in their efforts to create something different in music. But the "riding" trumpet, the "rippling" clarinet, and the "driving" trombone will always be symbolic of the music created by a people made free, giving expression to their emotions.

Jazz has influenced contemporary composers of serious music. Debussy, Gershwin, Stravinsky, Kurt Weill, Aaron Copland, and a great many others have used jazz themes, rhythms, and idioms as the basis of their compositions.

HOW HAS NEW ORLEANS JAZZ GAINED POPULAR RECOGNITION?

In the past several years the people in the United States have become increasingly interested in jazz. The improvised jazz of the New Orleans style has finally been recognized for what it is — a genuine folk music that is truly a part of our American folklore.

Since 1924, when Paul Whiteman gave the first jazz concert in Carnegie Hall and gently draped the mantle of respectability over jazz, we have come a long way in breaking down prejudices against jazz. Now, we take pride in presenting jazz festivals, where thousands of people can listen to the free improvisations of jazz musicians. Television and radio programs bring the true story of jazz into our homes. Recordings of jazz bands of the 1920's are being released again, and are considered choice collectors' items.

The American people have realized that jazz is a part of our musical heritage. In the words of Leonard Bernstein, one of America's outstanding composers and conductors, "We are showing a sensible acceptance of jazz as an art form that is emerging inevitably and nobly from the cultural development of our country."

The Band

THE BAND is composed of distinct sections: the *wood winds*, consisting of clarinets, oboes, bassoons, saxophones, flutes, and piccolos; the *brass winds*, made up of cornets, trumpets, trombones, and tubas; and the *percussion instruments*, comprising the kettledrums, bass and snare drums, triangles, and cymbals. Most bands differ from orchestras by not having a string section, although many concert bands include one or more string basses, a harp, and occasionally a cello.

The most important types of bands are the military and the concert band. Other kinds of bands are the jazz ensemble of wind and percussion instruments; the brass band, consisting of cornets, trumpets, trombones, saxophones, and drums; and some dance bands. Many so-called dance bands are really orchestras, since they include violins.

The military band is the model for the high school and college marching band. The number of players in such bands is usually small. Their primary purpose is to provide music

212

for parades, and for this reason the typical kind of music they play is the military march.

The concert band is only about sixty years old. In many ways it resembles a symphony orchestra. It plays many of the same compositions performed by an orchestra, and gives concerts from a stage or band shell. The players form a semicircle around the director, whose podium, like that of the orchestra conductor, is at the front and center of the stage. The seating arrangement of a concert band may vary, depending on the composition to be played, the acoustics of the hall, and other factors. As a general rule, however, the clarinets and flutes are seated nearest the director. Behind them are the saxophones and oboes, followed by the French horns, cornets, trumpets, and bassoons. At the rear of the platform are the percussion instruments, string basses, tubas, and trombones.

Seating Arrangement of a Concert Band

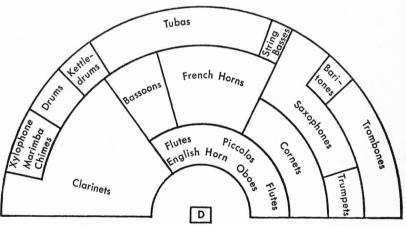

The Joliet (Ill.) Township High School Concert Band, 1959, Bruce H. Houseknecht, Conductor

The Symphony Orchestra

A LARGE symphony orchestra may have as many as 100 players, each of whom is an expert performer on his or her own instrument. It must contain a sufficient variety of instruments to sound every note in musical literature and be so well-trained and coordinated that it performs as if it were a single instrument played by the conductor.

The most important compositions performed by such an orchestra consist of symphonies, concertos (played in conjunction with soloists), oratorios (played in conjunction with a chorus), and tone poems, but it also plays shorter works such as suites, overtures, rhapsodies, waltzes, marches, and sometimes even popular melodies rewritten in symphonic form.

The modern symphony orchestra is composed of four divisions, or sections, and is seated in a semicircle around the conductor, whose podium is at the front and center of the concert stage. The four orchestra divisions are the strings, wood winds, the brass winds, and the percussion instruments.

The instruments of the string section consist of the first and second violins, the violas, the cellos, and the string basses. Except for the last, which are at the rear of the stage, the stringed instruments are nearest the conductor and carry the heaviest burden in most performances.

The wood winds, consisting of the flutes, piccolos, oboes, clarinets, bassoons, and English horns are seated behind the strings.

The brass winds, made up of trumpets, cornets, horns, trombones, and tubas give powerful harmonic support to passages in which the entire orchestra is playing together. They are the loudest melody instruments in the orchestra, and are usually placed behind the wood winds.

The percussion section maintains rhythm. It is composed of the timpani, snare drums, triangles, and cymbals, and is located at the rear of the concert stage.

Seating Arrangement of a Symphony Orchestra

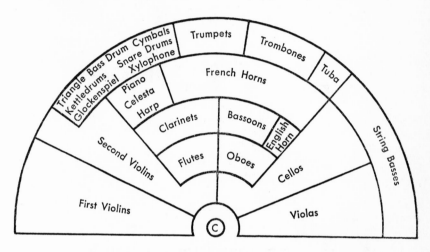

The Chicago Symphony Orchestra, Fritz Reiner, Music Director, 1959-60 concert season. Other orchestras have different seating arrangements. The location of the instruments of an orchestra may vary for several reasons. Among these are the acoustics of the hall and the requirements of the composition to be played.

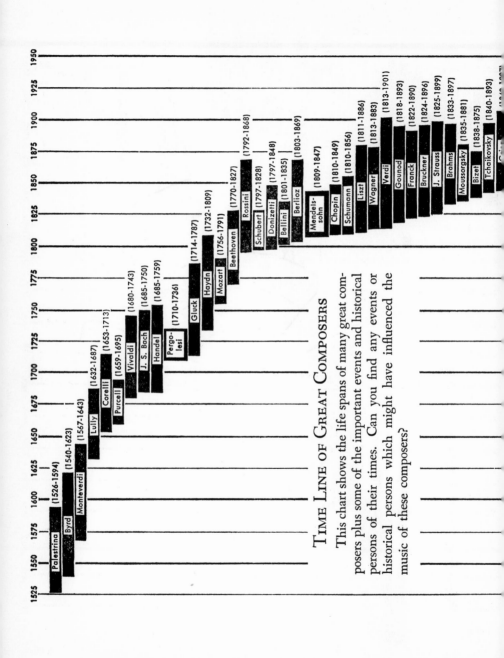

TIME LINE OF GREAT COMPOSERS

This chart shows the life spans of many great composers plus some of the important events and historical persons of their times. Can you find any events or historical persons which might have influenced the music of these composers?

Palestrina (1526-1594)

Byrd (1540-1623)

Monteverdi (1567-1643)

Lully (1632-1687)

Corelli (1653-1713)

Purcell (1659-1695)

Vivaldi (1680-1743)

J. S. Bach (1685-1750)

Handel (1685-1759)

Pergo-lesi (1710-1736)

Gluck (1714-1787)

Haydn (1732-1809)

Mozart (1756-1791)

Beethoven (1770-1827)

Rossini (1792-1868)

Schubert (1797-1828)

Donizetti (1797-1848)

Bellini (1801-1835)

Berlioz (1803-1869)

Mendels-sohn (1809-1847)

Chopin (1810-1849)

Schumann (1810-1856)

Liszt (1811-1886)

Wagner (1813-1883)

Verdi (1813-1901)

Gounod (1818-1893)

Franck (1822-1890)

Bruckner (1824-1896)

J. Strauss (1825-1899)

Brahms (1833-1897)

Moussorgsky (1835-1881)

Bizet (1838-1875)

Tchaikovsky (1840-1893)

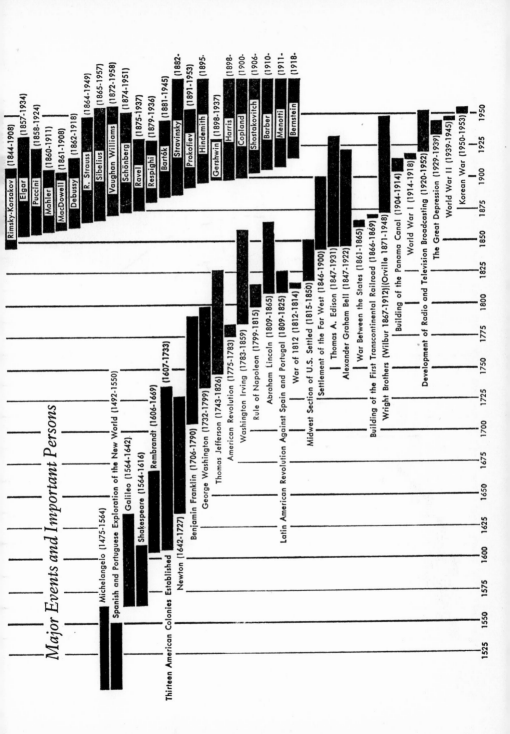

Major Events and Important Persons

Glossary of Musical Terms

A CAPPELLA (ä′kə·pel′ə) vocal music performed without the accompaniment of instruments.

ANTHEM a religious choral composition with words usually taken from the Scriptures. It may also be a patriotic song of praise and glory, such as a national anthem.

ARIA (ä′ri·ə) a composition for solo voice with instrumental accompaniment, performed as part of a longer work such as a cantata, oratorio, or opera.

ART SONG a song that has been deliberately composed for the purpose of expressing a particular mood. An art song differs from an aria by being an independent composition rather than part of a larger work, and from a folk song by being the creation of a professional composer.

BALLAD a popular song which repeats the same melody in each stanza.

BALLET a form of artistic dancing performed to specially composed music by a group of dancers on a stage. Ballets are presented in programs consisting of dances only, or as interlude and intermission entertainment in operas.

CADENZA (kə·den′zə) a brilliant solo passage usually inserted within a concerto or aria for the purpose of giving the soloist a chance to display his technical skills.

CANON (kan′ən) a strict repetition in quick succession of different voice or instrumental parts, as in a "round."

CANTATA (kən·tä′tə) a composition for soloists, chorus, and instrumental accompaniment. It consists of choruses, recitatives, arias, and duets, and has a text which tells a continuous story.

CAROL a traditional song, usually associated with Christmas.

CHAMBER MUSIC music composed for a small group of instrumentalists, such as a string trio or quartet. It is usually performed in a small auditorium or chamber.

CHORAL, CHORALE a sacred composition sung by a chorus.

CHORD a combination of three or more tones played simultaneously.

CHORUS a group of persons assembled for the purpose of singing together in harmony. It is also a part of a song, such as the refrain repeated at the end of each stanza.

CONCERTO (kən·cher'to) a composition for one, two, or more solo instruments and orchestra, usually in three movements.

CONCERTO GROSSO a composition in which a small group of instruments is played against a full orchestra.

COUNTERPOINT a style of composition in which two or more related melodies are played simultaneously.

DUET a composition for two voices or instruments.

FANTASIA (fan·tā'zhi·ə), **FANTASY** an instrumental composition with no set form.

FOLK SONG a song originating among the common people which has evolved to its present form through generations of usage. Folk songs tell stories about daily life and consist of many types, the most common being work songs, love songs, drinking songs, and patriotic songs. A few composed songs, such as Stephen Foster's "Old Kentucky Home," are often classified as folk songs because they have the qualities of folk music, but the vast majority of folk songs are of unknown origin.

FORM the arrangement of the parts of a musical composition into a definite pattern. Examples of musical forms are the sonata and the fugue.

FUGUE (fug) a composition that begins with a short melody performed by one voice or instrument which is then imitated by other voices or instruments following in close succession. As each of these repeats the theme at different intervals, their tones interweave into a single musical work.

HARMONY the artistic musical effect that results from the playing or singing of the notes of a chord at the same time. Harmony in compositions for such instruments as the piano and organ, and for orchestra or chorus, consists of the sounding of different chords together and in succession.

INCIDENTAL MUSIC instrumental music composed for performance during a play.

LIBRETTO (lə·bret'ō) the words of a cantata, oratorio, or opera.

MASS a composition for a capella chorus and soloists or for orchestra, chorus, and soloists, set to the text of the five main parts of the Roman Catholic church service.

MELODY a series of musical tones, related in key and rhythm, which form a tune.

MOVEMENT a major division in a long composition such as a symphony or string quartet.

MUSIC DRAMA a form of opera in which the music plays a more important part in telling the story than in ordinary operas.

MUSICAL COMEDY a play containing songs and dances that are tied together by a slender and comical plot.

MUSICAL PLAY a drama that uses music to help convey the story. In a really good musical play, the music is so well adjusted to the mood of the scene or the act in which it occurs that its performance, in the form of song or dance, seems perfectly natural to the audience.

OPERA a drama set to music for performance in a theater, using scenery, costumes, and stage acting. Among the musical forms it employs are the aria, recitative, and duet. In addition to soloists, a chorus and orchestra are also used.

OPERETTA a theatrical entertainment of light, sentimental character, in simple and popular style, containing spoken dialogue, music, and dancing.

OPUS a musical work or composition.

ORATORIO (ôr′ə·tô′ri·ō) a musical composition with a religious or secular text, usually performed in a concert hall. The music is frequently dramatic, although no scenery, costumes, or stage movements are used. The form is similar to, but longer than, that of the cantata.

OVERTURE an instrumental composition played at the beginning of such works as an oratorio, opera, or cantata.

PRELUDE an instrumental composition introducing a fugue, a suite, or the acts of an opera. The organ music that introduces a church service is also called a prelude.

QUARTET a composition for four solo voices or instruments.

RECITATIVE (res′ə·ta·tēv′) a musical setting of verse or prose which is sung in an oratorical manner. In opera this form is used for conversational purposes or for important narrations preceding an aria or chorus.

REQUIEM (rek′wi·əm) **REQUIEM MASS** a mass sung for the dead. The form is the same as the regular mass except that the joyful sections are replaced with more sorrowful music.

RHYTHM the regular succession of accented and unaccented tones.

220

SONATA (sə·nä′tə) a composition composed for performance by one or two instruments. It usually consists of three or four movements with different rhythms.

SONATA FORM the form or arrangement of the parts of a sonata. The first movement is usually *allegro,* meaning fast; the second is usually *andante,* or *largo,* meaning slow; the third, *scherzo,* is light and humorous; and the fourth, *finale* (the final movement) is most frequently bright and quick. The term *sonata form* refers also to the arrangement of the music in the first movement of a sonata, which consists of (1) *exposition,* in which a number of themes are introduced; (2) *development,* in which they are developed; and (3) *recapitulation,* in which they are repeated in a changed form.

SUITE (swēt) an instrumental composition consisting of either short, dance-like movements or a collection of descriptive pieces.

SYMPHONIC POEM (TONE POEM) a musical composition, usually in one movement, which is based on a poetic or descriptive idea.

SYMPHONY a sonata for orchestra. Like the sonata, the symphony is usually in four movements, but of much longer lengths.

TEMPO the rate of speed at which a composition is performed. The tempo can range from the slowest possible speeds to the fastest and is indicated by the composer. A slow tempo might be marked *largo, adagio,* or *lento;* a medium tempo, *andante,* or *moderato;* and a fast tempo, *allegro, presto,* or *prestissimo.*

THEME a short melody used as the basis of the sections of a musical composition such as a sonata, symphony, or opera.

THEME WITH VARIATIONS a musical form in which the original theme is repeated in a variety of ways.

224

3